A Journey Back

A JOURNEY BACK

Injustice and Restitution

❃

ARNON TAMIR

Translated by Ruth Hein
With an Afterword by Klaus Binder

NORTHWESTERN UNIVERSITY PRESS

Evanston, Illinois

Northwestern University Press
Evanston, Illinois 60208-4210

Originally published in German under the title *Eine Reise zurück: Von der Schwierigkeit Unrecht wiedergutzumachen.* Copyright © 1992 by Fischer Taschenbuch Verlag GmbH, Frankfurt am Main. English translation copyright © 1997 by Northwestern University Press. Published 1997. All rights reserved.

Printed in the United States of America

ISBN 0-8101-1186-1 (cloth)
ISBN 0-8101-1171-3 (paper)

Library of Congress Cataloging-in-Publication Data

Tamir, Arnon, 1917–
   [Reise zurück. English]
   A journey back : injustice and restitution / Arnon Tamir ; translated by Ruth Hein ; with an afterword by Klaus Binder.
      p. cm. — (Jewish lives)
   ISBN 0-8101-1186-1 (cloth : alk. paper). — ISBN 0-8101-1171-3 (pbk. : alk. paper)
      1. Tamir, Arnon, 1917– . 2. Jews—Germany—Stuttgart—Biography. 3. Jews—Germany—History—1933–1945. 4. Jews, German—Israel—Hazore'a—Biography. 5. Jews, German—Israel—Travel—Germany. I. Title. II. Series.
   DS135.G4S79713 1997
   943'.004924—dc21   97-9934
                                                                           CIP
                                                                           r97

Contents

A Journey Back

❀

A Leap in Time

At the southern border of our kibbutz, where the dry riverbed that meanders down from the mountains through the wooded slopes ends, lies the new swimming pool. We dug a large terrace out of the hillside and covered the dry, chalky soil with a lot of concrete and granulite. Around the pool itself, which we tiled in blue, we sowed grass for a lawn, and we planted flower beds. Palm trees now wave their fronds picturesquely where figs and olives used to grow. On summer days the people, young and old, all rush to this spot to cool off in the clear water. Early in the morning, when the sun rises over the hills of Nazareth to the east, the older members swim the marked laps from one end of the pool to the other, in the justified expectation that the activity will be good for body and soul. Around ten o'clock the teachers from the nursery schools and the lower grades bring their kids. The pool is full of children, the air echoes with happy shouts. During the afternoon the water becomes the province of the young foreigners who manage to combine work on the kibbutz with a vacation. Later, after work, whole families come, parents with their children—even the littlest ones, who splash around in a wading pool of their own. And the young people are everywhere, showing off their skills in bold dives, flexing their muscles as they toss a ball back and forth. They race across the grass, dodging between the lawn chairs scattered about, where young women, our guests from northern climes, let the sun turn their skin brown.

When I've had enough of the water, I also lie in one of the chairs to bask in the sun's warmth. And maybe I'll close my eyes, maybe I'll listen to the voices around me and to the echo from the hillside across from us. I can almost believe that I'm entitled to enjoy the here and now, the way the world looks and sounds at this moment. What's past is past. I have every right to retire. But that's not how it works.

I open my eyes to gaze at the hillside of green spruces, on the other side of the valley. Some of my old friends seem to line up before my eyes, as clear as day. They are still young, they are dressed in khaki trousers and shirts, some of them are bareheaded, others are wearing gray caps. They strike at the brambles with the hoes they hold in their hands. Here and there boulders rise up through the brush. A young girl in shorts walks up, leading a donkey loaded down with water canisters; the animal clumsily scrambles up the slope among the rocks. The water has been hauled from the gully to irrigate the saplings being planted on the hill. The donkey stumbles and keels over, and the canisters fall with the beast. The water, which has been brought here with so much trouble and difficulty, flows over the parched and arid soil. The group's laughter rings all the way to where I am. Or am I hearing the echo of our voices bounce back from the slope? Is today's joyful noise an echo of the laughter from that other time?

At this moment I cannot remember precisely whether I ever really saw the row of laboring men on the desolate mountainside or whether it is merely a hallucination. And in my mind's eye I see the photograph that hangs in the little museum we established in an old watchtower, the memorial to the earliest years of our settlement. But how was I supposed to tell the difference, without getting confused, between those things I actually lived and the stories others tell over and over to our sons and grandsons? The farther away we get from the past, the more we comply with the duty of telling our descendants about the events of long ago, the more fanciful our stories grow; we may hush up some of what happened or disregard certain events. That's why the old-timers keep starting the same conversations about what happened in the past, what exactly took place. So we remember and we forget, both at the same time. And when we think about the past, each of us remembers something different. But some time ago there was a village on this hillside, right where we dug the deep pit to build a swimming pool always filled with fresh water. It was a tiny, godforsaken nest, a few squat stone shanties and smoky mud huts. The Arabs who were our neighbors sat outside their doors and stared in astonishment and disbelief at our friends toiling on the opposite slope in the burning heat of the sun to change the world order. Early in the morning, as we did every day, we went out from our tents and rickety wooden shacks, which stood far below in the valley, to plant trees in the mountain wilderness—in the steadfast faith that we were creating something new, something that had never existed before. Our neighbors sat on this side of the gully, right where I'm sitting now. Their village was called Kiri. They were tenant farmers. They leased and worked the land in the valley; we had bought these acres for cash on the barrelhead and at inflated prices from landowners who lived in Beirut and Damascus. We got the money from our parents, who had stayed behind in Germany. After all, we had come to this land with practically empty hands, just as it said in one of the songs we used to sing:

With nothing we came, they say,
Escaping the poverty of yesterday.

But paying the owners wasn't the last of it. They did not honor the agreement to indemnify their tenants, our neighbors in Kiri. So, after lengthy negotiations, every family had to be compensated all over again. In the course of time, about half the villagers, thanks to these settlements, moved to land of their own and into stone houses on the other side of the valley. The other half, those who chose to drag out the negotiations, stayed in the village. Perhaps they hoped to wangle a bigger payout. Or they might have had other reasons. Of course there's no way to truly remember all the details of something that happened such a long time ago, but there's no doubt whatever that our Arab neighbors were at home in the same spot where at this very moment I'm resting from my labors and that on the opposite hillside we were uprooting thistles and brambles and planting trees. At all times of day they followed these peculiar goings-on, took note of every new tent we pitched and every new wooden hut we built within the confines of our kibbutz. I'm sure they counted the sheep and chickens we kept in primitive sheds. Who knows what went through their minds as they watched a new settlement growing before their eyes. No one could imagine at the time what would happen later.

Filtered through the voices of our sons and daughters—who by now have established families of their own and at this instant are busily coaxing their pride and joy out of the chilly water before they catch cold—I can hear a discussion that took place in the kibbutz not too long ago. That time we, the older generation, let the young people convince us that, now that nearly fifty years had gone by since the kibbutz's founding, the time had come to build a proper swimming pool. And we agreed to pay for this innovation with money the older members had received from the German government as compensation for persecution and expulsion, for the loss of family property, and for so much more that money can't buy. All this money flows into the kibbutz's general funds. The younger generation sees it as a kind of horn of plenty, but for all those who had to emigrate or were displaced and whose families perished in the Holocaust, money cannot undo what was done. However much money may flow from there to us, it will not dry up the sea of tears.

Thus, on this lawn by the swimming pool all the threads that have gone into weaving my story become tied into a single knot: we over there, on the hillside, struggling to cultivate the wilderness by the sweat of our brow; our neighbors on this side of the valley, who either moved away or fled at a later time; and the money that comes from Germany to make amends for what is irretrievably lost. Another thread that weaves through the story is the fate of the large village of Abu-Sorek, situated east of the kibbutz, on the far side of the mountain across the valley.

And finally: there is myself, trying to unravel the tangle in which our destinies are snarled so that I can tell an orderly, truthful story. Not such an easy task, to tell the truth about the past, since truth has many faces. It was not always thus. There was a time when truth had but a single face, smooth and neatly structured, like the facade of a brand-new building. It was clear to see that the old order had passed, and rightly so. There was only one truth: today and tomorrow. And so we sang:

> Our reward: the future of all those we hold dear,
> Yesterday's gone, tomorrow is already here.

By now the today and the tomorrow of that time has already turned into yesterday. And all that happened in between hardly resembles the smooth, firm facade of a new building. The cracks show.

They say that it's a sign of old age when you start to see or hear something else in everything, something that is hidden, a kind of double or threefold perception occurring simultaneously. I developed that trait early on, somewhere around the end of the 1950s. Until then my life was divided into two equal parts. At the age of twenty-one I was driven from Germany in an easterly direction. Another twenty-one years passed before I approached the borders of that country again. This time I was coming from the south. In the second half of my life—by now it is no more than a third—I made every effort to forget the first half. I was busy, along with my friends, building a home for us, for our families, and for everyone willing to live and work with us. There was so much to be planned and done that we felt little need to think about the past. It seemed to have sunk into the obscurity of forgetfulness. If the past nevertheless rose up now and then, I did all I could to push the memory back, as if I wanted to repel an enemy army that was marching through the African desert toward our destruction.

❈

Return

Europe, where we grew up, threw us out. In my head and my heart I felt cut off from the past and from the country that expelled me. But if one of us steps on European soil now, after twenty years, he's no longer a Jewish refugee but a citizen of his own nation, confident and self-assured, feet firmly planted on the ground of reality.

On my way I had a stopover in Athens. I climbed up to the Acropolis, and there I first felt the slight tremor rising from the firm ground under my feet. I was standing between the columns of the Parthenon, a little blinded by the rays of the setting sun, lost in admiration of the creative courage of those who had built this masterpiece. After all, I'd spent many years as a builder myself, and I had some inkling of the mysteries of architecture. Beside a toppled capital I saw the silhouette of a lecturer. And the sound of his voice, husky with pipe smoke, was enough to let me recognize my old high-school teacher at once. Freedom of thought, I hear him say, has its origins in Athens. Slaves are not capable of expressing their thoughts. It took a noble people to create the civilization that was the cradle of our civilization. In a manner of speaking, we are all sons of Athens. . . .

Rowdy students in the classroom. *He* has gone. The noise level rises.

A cheerful class, boys and girls running about among the columns while a young teacher takes great pains, speaking a language I can't understand, to explain to them the principles of Hellenic architecture. I spend a long time walking along the worn flagstones, looking at the wondrous blocks of stone that, one placed on top of another, form a new entity, the columns with their long fluting, tapering off toward the top. I feel small when confronted with this spirit. The teacher clears his throat to dislodge the smoker's mucus. "A true, aristocratic race . . . they did the planning, and slaves did the actual

7

work. That is the order that obtained in that world. Backward people can bring only inferior cultures into being . . . ." The outline of his body stands between me and the sun. He says something else, but his words are drowned in the roaring engines of an airplane flying overhead in the clear blue sky.

The airplane floats high above dazzling white clouds, luminous in the light of the autumn sun. The voice of the captain, coming over the loudspeakers on board, informs us that we are about to fly over the German border. Slowly we dive down into the clouds and glide along, swathed in white cotton. No sky above us now. Impossible to see what lies below. All around us thick, impenetrable fog—it is a grayish white, thickish emulsion, which my mother feeds me twice a day by the spoonful. "It's good for you," she says. "The doctor says cod-liver oil works wonders." You've got to be big and strong, stronger than the others. Around her neck she wears a tiny, blood-red ruby that dangles from a thin chain. The stone is embedded in a dainty flower of silver filigree. I close my eyes, swallow the fishy emulsion that will make me strong. I hear a voice at my side. Someone, speaking German, says, "Have you ever in your life seen such fog? Russia is the only place I ever saw fog this thick."

"I live in Israel," I reply tersely. I really don't want to go on with this conversation.

"Oh." He's surprised. "That doesn't matter at all. Really it doesn't."

I have absolutely no interest in talking to this man, but he will not let it go. He introduces himself; he's a salesman for a big German firm. He is well groomed. A golden pin glitters at the center of his necktie, his nails are manicured. He must be about my age. He's been in Russia—probably in the army.

"It really doesn't matter," he repeats. Why?

I withdraw into myself and try to concentrate on whatever it is that is waiting for me down there, below the blanket of clouds.

"But you really speak German very well." His curiosity overcomes his embarrassment.

"I was born here . . . ." I don't really want to talk to him, but I do.

"Oh, yes . . . . Of course." Finally he lets go. Grayish white light forces its way through the windows.

"We've reached the border," he mumbles, more or less to himself.

I look out the window. I can see the sooty walls of the station gliding slowly past. We stop. The carriages bump together gently as the train comes to a final stop.

"We're at the border. Poland is on the other side," someone next to me murmurs.

Outside there is shouting. "Let's go, hurry up . . . Jews out of the cars!" Policemen in uniform, armed with carbines, and police detectives in civilian clothing run up and down the platform screaming at us, each one of them an all-powerful potentate who holds our fate in his hands. Very early in the morning a policeman had appeared at the apartment we shared and, in the name of the city's chief of police, handed me a printed form ordering my immediate deportation. War was already in the air, but peace still reigned. "You don't have to take anything with you," the policeman said. "It's purely a formality. You'll be back home by evening."

Nevertheless, my friends secretly tuck a few bills into my coat pocket. It is five o'clock in the morning. The policeman leads me through the empty streets of the sleeping city. None of this really came as a surprise. So why do I feel indignant and insulted?

"Hand over any cash you have on you! Anyone who holds back money illegally will be killed on the spot!" Several hundred Jews stand on the platform, most of them in the prime of life, family men who, like myself, were hauled out of bed even before the first light of day and transported to the frontier. In the blink of an eye they have been turned into refugees, into pitiful, miserable nonpersons. Some hand over whatever money they have. The locomotive across from me gives off great cloudy puffs of steam that rise to the sooty roof of the railroad station and from there float off into the night. In the distance, a few shots.

"Really interesting. They used to say that the Jews are shrewd businessmen but miserable soldiers," my seatmate says. With undisguised admiration he adds, "Today you'd think just the opposite. A miracle, what you people accomplished during your war of independence against the superior strength of the Arab forces!"

Shreds of fog everywhere. On a slight rise in the hillside a tiny stone house comes into view, a few olive trees next to it. There's also a fig tree. A fellah is nestled against the wall, his back is to us, he seeks the cover of the corner. In his hand is a gun with a long barrel. Now he aims around the corner in the direction of the mountain.

There, in the fog, tiny figures run from rock to rock. The crack of gunfire rings out, and you can see tiny bolts of lightning flare at the end of the black tubes they hold in their hands. Bangs spray sparks from an exhaust. The airplane loses altitude. A long whistle fills the cabin.

"The main thing is to get there in one piece," my seatmate mutters. "You hear so many stories . . . ."

My eyes meet those of the train's engineer, who is looking down at us from his stall. His face, smeared with soot, is inscrutable, as if he were used to watching while others do the job of expelling. He turns to speak to the stoker over his shoulder. The stoker opens the boiler door, stares into the fire, spits into the flames with care and deliberation, lets the door bang shut again. Additional uniforms emerge out of the night's darkness. Some hold leather leashes by which they lead panting dogs, their long tongues hanging out. They are German shepherds, man's best friend. Customs officers are also suddenly among us: "Open your bags! Inspection!"

They are still rummaging among the pieces of clothing that had been stuffed hurriedly into bundles and valises; they are carefully and deliberately marking the lids with white chalk crosses as a sign that the inspection has been completed when another loudspeaker blares: "Line up by fours! And step on it! Faster! Faster!"

Startled, those who are being expelled seek to obey the command and find their place. The confusion grows. One of the uniforms shouts with thunderous contempt: "Damned scumbags! Where do you think you are—in your own stinking Jew quarters?"

Finally we leave the railroad station, a column of bent and submissive men. Using their dogs, they drive us into the main street of the little border town. The street is paved with cobblestones. An old man stumbles, drops his suitcase. A young guy in uniform picks up the case and helps the old man back onto his feet and into line. When he feels the eyes of his fellows on him, he quickly presses the suitcase back in the old man's hand, claps him lightly on the shoulder as if to encourage him, and walks along the row of men to the front. We are marching along between two rows of houses that appear, in the pale light of the gas lamps, like solid gray walls. The shutters are closed over the windows, but we can sense that there are people behind them. Perhaps they are sitting at tables set with linen and china, having their supper. Perhaps not. They have been forbidden to ask questions, and they obey. The war, even if it has not yet been officially declared, changes the measure of all things, an order is an order.

"Is this your first trip back after . . . I mean, after everything that's happened in all these years?" He starts in on me again. I mutter something or other to myself.

"It's not so simple. Great parts of the city have been destroyed. . . . And to meet your old neighbors again—if they've survived the war—you must be pretty excited. I imagine. Not simple at all. The war changed everything. . . ."

Some of our neighbors from the village of Abu-Sorek, which is situated east of the kibbutz, are brought into our courtyard as the first prisoners of a war that is never officially declared. Shocked and shaken, we circle around them. We could have lived peaceably side by side, they and us, until the end of time. In a row, one after the other, they are led through the courtyard, in their cloaks and shabby shoes. Farmers, just like us. None of us can imagine that anyone who has lived here for generations will not return to his own house.

The column slowly drags itself out of the little town. Here, in the open country, the road is no longer paved, there is only damp and slippery soil in which the wagon wheels have dug deep ruts. Like a long caterpillar, the column of men creeps to the raised barrier that marks the border and from there into no-man's-land. Soldiers stand beside the road, gathered around a machine gun. A young officer waves his hands wildly: "Come along, straight ahead, get going! And don't even think about coming back!" The column with a thousand feet disappears into the night fog. A soft sigh rises to the sky, which is shrouded in black clouds.

Raindrops. The rain grows heavier. We roll onto the shiny landing strip. A low building topped with a tower faces us. A woman's voice over the loudspeaker: "Welcome to Stuttgart. Thank you for flying with us." Her voice is followed by sentimental music.

※

Arrival

The plane taxis to a stop. It seems to me that I can hear a sigh of relief at the smooth landing. The passengers make ready to deplane. My seatmate wishes me a pleasant stay before pushing his way toward the door. I remain glued to my seat and stare at the tower. I am still sitting here, lost in thought, with all the places and all the times within me. I have not yet arrived, not yet. I have to go outside now and cross the black expanse where heavy raindrops splash and spatter. It has to be. There is no going back, not in time and not in place.

A young border guard examines my Israeli passport. Of course he opens it from the wrong side. Stamp. Not a word. From here to the customs official in his green uniform. Why am I so nervous? He asks politely, "Have you anything to declare?"

I look at him, dismayed. My eyes grow moist. I wasn't prepared for that. I must have expected him to shout, "Anyone who holds on to illegal money will be killed on the spot!"

"I'm from Israel," I stutter.

A broad smile spreads across his face. "But of course. Everything's in order."

Carefully and deliberately he chalks a white cross on the lid of my suitcase. The official act completed, he wishes me a pleasant stay.

The bus that is to take us into town drives through the woods. The trees are glorious in autumnal red and yellow. Everything is both familiar and strange. Rustling through the leaves that cover the ground, throwing them up into the air, my friends' happy shouts. . . . Standing barefoot in a little stream and building a dam of stones and twigs. Playing volleyball in a sun-drenched clearing between green trees, picking blackberries among the shrubbery, later sitting with the others around the campfire, staring into the flickering flames while we all sing:

Brothers, to the sun, to freedom . . . .

We slept on the ground, in an improvised sleeping bag that Mother sewed, using a blanket. We dreamed of an everlasting land of youth. In the middle of the night you wake up and listen to the menacing voices of the forest. This is where it was. No, over there. Don't think about it!

The paved road leads out of the wood, and below, in the valley, the city comes into view, the sea of roofs, church spires towering over them, as if nothing had changed. War or no war. The rain has stopped. The wet roofs glitter in the light of thin sunbeams. We drive slowly down into the valley. On both sides of the road lie vineyards, the pride of the city. Country houses, surrounded by stone walls, stand as they used to. The bombs apparently fell farther down, at the center of the city. I see myself climbing the steep steps leading up the hillside, ringing the bells at garden gates, knocking on front doors, holding out the brightly painted box: a donation for our German brothers abroad. Here, in the hilly vineyards of Stuttgart, the world still looks pretty whole and unscathed. The bus drives down into the city. Streetscapes return in memory. Here and there a house is missing. The bus stops at the railroad station. I know the square again, and at the same time I do not know it. The station—an edifice of gray stone that was once considered the crowning glory of modern architecture—is missing a wing. Across from the station a large crane juts from a huge gaping hole in the ground. A hideous crater at the heart of the city. The day of judgment, apocalypse.

Galloping between the ruined houses, along abandoned paths, donkeys moving swiftly along under fig trees and pomegranate trees, which have been abandoned to their fate. Their pounding hooves stir up clouds of dust that come to lie heavy on the soul.

Here there is the roar of jackhammers that tear open the earth, preparing it to receive the foundations of new buildings, an earsplitting noise in the principal street. Commercial buildings rise anew, not made of stone or brick and gussied up with ornamental plaster and stucco and topped with steep roofs, as was the fashion at the end of the nineteenth century. No, what is being created here are cubes of steel and glass. Rows of shop windows cheek by jowl.

White slogans are daubed on some of the glass panes. Men in brown uniforms stand holding signs. Others block access to the doors.

When Jewish blood spurts from the knife,
Our life is twice as sweet . . . .

Passersby stop and, in silence, watch the goings-on. A woman in slovenly clothes pushes her way through the uniforms, utters some kind of oath, and disappears into the store. There's no point in standing outside the shop any longer. My father will not be coming. The names on the shop signs have disappeared as well. Bamberger, Herz, Levy, Salberg, Wolf. New names, new owners.

Through many long nights we debated what should happen to our neighbors' property piled up in our courtyard: plows, tools, other stuff. Finally we agreed to sell the things and use the proceeds to acquire more weapons to expand our meager arsenal before the forces of the Arab states invaded our land. The thought of enriching ourselves personally never occurred to us. "Ill-gotten gains never prosper!" How absurd they are, these sayings that dog us. After all, I am supposed to procure statements from witnesses in this city in which my parents were deprived of what little property they had. And I am supposed to pursue the claims that have been submitted in my name.

The hotel is in the street where the offices of the Jewish community once stood, near the big synagogue. At the place where you turn into this street, they are renovating the steeple of the Protestant church. A workman stands high up on the scaffolding, fitting gilded hands on the black dial with the Roman numerals, which are gilded as well. The punctiliously reconstructed church is almost the only older building left in the street. Across from the little hotel, which wasn't here before, stands the rebuilt synagogue. I look across the street at the whitewashed cube with three tall, narrow windows and, in front of the building, the small tiled courtyard with a round water basin. Above the entrance I can make out the Hebrew words: "Open the gates and let the righteous and faithful enter." The letters are remarkably large.

Behind the new synagogue looms the old one. At the front of the flat roof, between the arabesques of the border, are set the Tablets of the Law. Behind them the lead-trimmed dome rises high. At its tip the Star of David points the way to heaven. Arch-bearing columns fit snugly into the facade of rough-hewn gray stone. The synagogue, built in the Moorish style, is a hybrid, a mixture of church and mosque. A vaulted niche holds the Ark of the Covenant. Varicolored panes fill the round windows on both sides. The sunbeams that fall through them into the building's interior paint a mosaic of red and yellow squiggles on the marble floor, sliding over the rows of brown pews where a little flock of boys and girls are sitting, I among them. A bearded rabbi, on his head a black cap with a square brim like that of a university professor, a prayer shawl embroidered with silver threads covering his shoulders, delivers the sermon. I stare upward into the high space, up to the dome painted with vines and leaves; at the very center a large gilded chandelier glitters with candle-shaped bulbs. The palace of Harun al-Rashid, the mysteries of a distant land to the East. A red velvet curtain hangs in front of the sanctuary. Two lions, embroidered in silver, hold a crown. The door to the Holy of Holies is opened. The cantor sings strange modulations and lifts out the Torah scroll; little bells hang from its silver crown. The tinny ringing makes me shiver. Sentimental organ sounds float above the top hats of the prominent members of the congregation. The elegantly dressed wives and daughters look down from the women's gallery. The service is over, and everybody rushes through the city streets toward home. The Jewish holiday falls on an ordinary weekday, and it is important to remain as inconspicuous as possible. The trusty custodian, who is not Jewish, locks the black grating at the gate, which is surmounted by the words "So sayeth God: You are all my children." Chiseled into the gray stone, for all eternity.

"What did they do with the stones?" I ask the reedy hotel owner. He gives me a look of total incomprehension. Or perhaps he does understand me but prefers not to answer. Could be that he's used to Jewish guests, returning for brief visits, asking peculiar questions. Some time or other I heard a story that after the synagogue was burned down, farmers from around the city came and loaded the sooty stones onto their horse-drawn carts and carried them off to the countryside, where they used them to build retaining walls in the vineyards. According to another version, no one was willing to touch them.

For a long time the houses stood empty and abandoned. Scorpions and snakes crawled through them, a danger to our children, who roamed freely among the decaying walls to pick figs and pomegranates. The word was, "If you don't take the stones for your own buildings or to pave the road, there's plenty of others who will." I wasn't convinced. Later, bulldozers came along and cleared the slope for an orchard. Only one small building remained standing, farther down in the valley, near the road, the tomb of a sheikh—to tell the world that once a village stood here.

I put my suitcase on the bed without opening it, telephone the woman who was a friend of my parents in antediluvian times, and make an appointment. I will call on her at once. I also telephone the agency that deals with restitution of expropriated Jewish property; the same office also investigates claims for compensation for things that cannot be restored. Although I have an appointment for the following morning, I try to move it up to this afternoon. A polite male voice informs me that the lady who is investigating my case has not come in to work today but that she will certainly see me the following morning, as arranged. But in case she turns up in the office today after all, he will tell her that I called, he promises me, and if my appointment can be moved up, she will leave a message at the hotel. Even as he is talking, I suddenly realize that under no circumstances will I spend the night in this place, in this city.

Old Paths, Old Neighbors

I leave the hotel as quickly as I can and go on my way without another look at the new, squat synagogue across the street. My feet carry me through streets that are somehow familiar. I pass along them like a sleepwalker. Quite by chance—I could just as easily have turned into a different street—I take the route to my old high school. On the large square before the entrance some students are horsing around under the chestnut trees. Everything is just as it used to be. Nothing is as it used to be. The menacing gray stone facade of the school remains, but between the stones there is now the gleam of yellow clinkers, which I don't remember and which seem strangely inappropriate. The bells of the nearby Catholic church, which still stands in all its glory, ring out, loud and sure. A covert glance through the classroom window to the round clock dial on the church tower. In the background I hear a voice, it belongs to all of them at once—the elementary-school teacher Herr Kober; Herr Sieber, who drilled Latin into us; Herr Schmitthenner, who taught in the school and who proudly sported dueling scars on his face, railed against the republic, and was given to recounting his army experiences during the war whenever we succeeded in distracting him from his lesson plan; and the physics instructor Herr Kessel, a peculiar bachelor who was said to harbor inappropriate feelings for students and who later was to commit suicide. Their voices merge with murmurs, with little coughs, with twanging sounds; if you had them all on tape, you could play them backward as easily as forward without its making any appreciable difference. I see all the sides of the church, too, all at the same time. The overly large entrance portal stands open, as always. A massive gloomy space tempts and frightens with its dimmed lights and strange odors. The entrance at the back of the church is always locked. Set in a recess, it is in deep shade and is provided with an

19

iron grating on which artful cast-iron leaves are entwined. Large tubs with ferns and palms stand in the twilit niche. You can feel the damp warmth of the lush flora of faraway places. On the broad stairs leading up to the locked gate a bunch of first-year students is arranged for a group portrait; those in the back row are standing behind a row of seated boys and another row who are kneeling. The teacher, in his full height, rises above the heads sporting military crewcuts; his arms are majestically folded across his chest. He wears a little beard. His head is propped up by a stiff collar and yet trembles and wobbles now and then, the consequence of a disability incurred in the war. His facial muscles are strained and taut from his valiant efforts to hold his head still, and his eyes have a rigid, severe expression. Herr Kober, the elementary-school teacher who has become the music teacher in the high school, beloved and feared at the same time. I look into my eyes, which stare at me from the photograph outside the church, I see my round head, my shorn crown, my full lips that are always parted a little. And I listen intently to the words of the photographer, who is pushing the square plate into the large instrument on the wooden tripod. "Pay attention, people! Watch the birdie!" And he's gone, disappeared underneath the black cloth, his outstretched hand holds the button, and he puts on an alluring voice to count: "One . . . two . . . ." I am in these eyes, I am these great, brown eyes that look at me expectantly. Any moment now the bird will dart out of the black folds behind the lens. My life will flutter up to heaven, the home of God, who watches over us.

When at night I go to sleep,
Fourteen angels watch do keep . . .

" . . . and three!" Click. For a split second, the blank glass eye of the lens.

God's deputy on earth, Herr Kober, teacher, lines us up by twos and leads us back into the school. He dispenses praise and blame, reward and blame, with an inscrutable feeling for justice. Sometimes, as a sign of approbation, he pinches a student's cheek or benevolently gives his earlobe a little tweak. At other times his right hand wields his pliant cane and brings it whizzing down on the hand or the behind of the student who is stretched out on the first desk, in front of the class, while the teacher's left hand, with an expert grip, stretches the seat of the sinner's trousers.

There is no appeal from the canings, beatings were *ultima ratio*, a hard-learned lesson. In the square outside the school the boys form a circle around the fighting cocks and egg them on with enthusiastic shouts, addressed especially to my adversary: "Let him have it! He's scared shitless, the Jewboy!" A damp film clouds my eyes. "Fight back. Give two, three times as good as you got," says my father. "Show him that you're not afraid. If somebody hits you, you hit back, even if he's bigger than you." Opposite me stands someone who is bigger than I am. Some of my friends are among the boys who form the outer circle. They are cautiously waiting to see how things will turn out. I stand there with clenched fists, ready to hang a hook on my adversary's chin. He doesn't move, he merely winks at someone behind me. Before I know what's happening, a hail of blows crashes down on me from the back. Blind with angry tears, I kick out in every direction, filled with humiliation at the sneak attack; it's as if the rules established for boys' fights do not apply to me. Shouting in triumph, the crowd of boys, my friends among them, scatters. Some call to me from the distance: "What a crybaby! He's yellow!" I am left alone and abandoned on the square. Tears of helplessness run down my cheeks still stinging from the blows they've received. One boy comes back, picks up my satchel from where it has fallen to the ground, and hands it to me. He is not one of my friends. He says, "What a shitty thing to do," and goes on his way. And now I stand in the circle of boys around two fighting cocks. I follow the menacing gestures that lead up to the fight proper, the fight that will break out at any moment. I search for familiar faces. Even in calmer times it could happen that they called insults at your back as you were walking down the road below the village. They threw stones, too. We had learned that we had to call out, in Arabic, *"Wen il abbuk, ja wallad?"* ("Hey, kid, where's your father?"). That got rid of them. There was the uneasy feeling that the laws of the civilized world did not apply to us.

The church bells are still tolling as I slowly climb the steps that lead to the entrance of the high school. I go into the lobby. To my left and my right the busts of Homer and Virgil stare down at me. Homer's nose is smeared with India ink. I had specialized in drawing black mustaches. Behind the busts marble tablets, set into the wall, display the engraved names of the students who gave their lives for the Fatherland in the First World War. Several dozen names are there, faded to a reddish tint. Where is the tablet with the names of my fellow students who lost their lives in the Second World War? I ought to care. I climb the stairs to the second floor, where the office is, and I come to a stop before a door with a glass insert. The pane of glass is new. My heart is beating wildly. I give a timid knock. Behind the door the principal, Professor Kutschenreuter, who always wears a frock coat and a high, stiff collar with a neat bow tie, is waiting for me. He is enthroned behind the broad expanse of his desk. Some writing pads lie on the green blotter next to the inkwell. For a long time he looks at me over his half-glasses, runs his hand over his bristly head, where each hair stands upright like a brush. After a while he carefully smooths his tie.

"It is only on the recommendation of your former teacher, Herr Kober, that we are refraining from expelling you," he says, his voice even and calm. What trouble have I got into this time? Probably broke a couple of windows while horsing around. Or used a crib sheet during a test. Or forged my father's signature on an excuse, created a disturbance in class . . . .

"Can I help you?" asks the young woman seated behind a desktop of veneered plywood held up by a structure of chrome blocks. Her gaze is candid and straightforward, a little curious. I try to explain myself and don't quite know what to say. I'm not at all certain what I'm doing here. I ask her for a list of names of the school's former students; I explain that I too attended the school and left it in the year of national renewal for obvious reasons, that I've just come from Israel. The names of long-forgotten schoolmates rise to the top of my memory: Spengler, tall and blond; Sommer, whose father was a high-ranking officer in the army; Götz, the top student in our class, who did things with women and became a man overnight. . . .

"Oh," she says, "I see," without batting an eyelash. A moment of silence. Then she collects herself. "No problem," she says. She rises and turns to the metal cabinet along the wall behind her. With the sure movements of a woman who has no problem with requests like mine, she begins to explore its contents. I send still more names in the direction of her back. "Geissenberg. Merz. Dietrich. Waidmann. Benzinger."

Benzinger, the bully. He plants himself in front of me, his legs spread wide, sporting his brown uniform. Lately the teachers have become lenient when students transgress school regulations that forbid the wearing of uniforms in school. Benzinger's father owns a stationery store that barely ekes out a living, he is always on the edge of bankruptcy; the shop is situated very near the flourishing multistoried department store that has a Jewish name. Benzinger was always one of the slowest in our class, and there was no denying that he was more than a little dense; he just barely managed to get promoted each year.

"Jews don't work! It's a known fact!" he announces loudly and holds out to me a piece of cardboard in the shape of a ticket. In big capital letters it reads, "To PALESTINE. ONE WAY TICKET."

"I can't wait for the day when we finally get a look at your backside!" he sneers. He's taller than me by a head, overfed and spoiling for a fight. He looks around proudly; yesterday the class dummy, a favorite butt of ridicule, today he is king. Once again my eyes mist over. With sudden energy I take one step toward him, ready to fight with him as I've become used to doing through all these years. Surprised, he draws back and pulls brass knuckles from his pocket. "Another step, and you're dead meat." At that moment several other students enter the fray; these boys form a kind of elite in the eyes of their classmates. It was said of one of them that outside school he wears a black uniform; another boy comes from a noble family. They haul Benzinger off to a corner: "Are you nuts? That's not the way to fight the Jews," they declare with certainty.

Then they turn to me. "We've got nothing against you personally. You've always been one of us, that's not going to change."

I'm having trouble digesting this announcement. For years they had deliberately avoided becoming friendly with me, and at this time of all times a sense of decency and chivalry is born in their hearts? "The struggle against international Jewry is a colossal effort, it's the grown-ups' business, not ours." And to prove that they are quite capable of making a distinction between world Jewry and me, they seek me out more frequently from then on, they even ask me to their homes. For years I've waited for this moment, and when it comes, the strange offers of friendship leave me cold. I left school even before the year was out.

For a split second I wonder why I remember only the disagreeable events of my school years. There must have been teachers whose classes I enjoyed, the same way I enjoyed school outings in Swabia's magnificent countryside. But other memories rush in on me, kindle my anger, torment me, burn. Over and over a person whose love was rejected relives the affront.

"Everything is on the record," says the young secretary and pushes a pamphlet toward me. "Here you'll find the names of the students and faculty for every year, their addresses, too. Not all of them, of course."

"My elementary-school teacher, Herr Kober, came to the high school as the music teacher. Is he still alive?"

She leafs through the folder. "Here is his address. He retired long ago."

She places the pamphlet between us on the desk. "Is there anything else?" Now she smiles wanly and adjusts her blouse. She has pretty breasts.

Without thinking about it, I say, "Were the yellow clinkers on the front of the building always there?" Before I can add, "It's in the worst taste," she answers casually, "The bombings did a lot of damage to the building. Probably they wanted to renovate it somewhat. Doesn't make much sense to keep the old without making changes, does it?"

"Of course . . . absolutely." I try to tear my eyes away from her blouse.

"Perhaps you'd like to leave us your address in Israel? Sometimes one of our former students comes here, just as you have, to look for former classmates . . . ," she lowers her voice, "if, that is, they're still alive . . . ."

Somebody opens the glass door and lets it fall shut again without entering. A crack like a shot. The pane of glass rattles.

"Thanks. I'll think about it," I say in leaving. The struggle against international Jewry is a colossal effort, it's the grown-ups' business, not ours. What would Sommer and gangly Spengler say today if they hadn't died in the war?

"What shall we do when greater ones than ourselves go over our heads and make war against you?" The village elder of Abu-Sorek phrases his answer with care. A delegation from the kibbutz has come to speak with him. In his house we are seated on mattresses spread on the bare concrete floor around a small stove in which charcoal is burning. A finjan with very black, very sweet coffee sits atop the little stove. From time to time our host fans the air with a piece of sheet metal. The stream of air sets the coals aglow until the fire dies down again. There are only men in the room. The voices of the women and children can be heard outside. We can also hear the cackle of free-ranging chickens, now and again accompanied by the bray of a donkey or the lowing of a cow from the shed around the corner. The men sit across from each other in two half circles, on one side the fellahin in full black capes or in thin jackets of dark material. Under these they wear white trousers that billow into a kind of sack between their legs. Their heads are topped by white kaffiyehs. They are old, their faces are lined, their mustaches are white. Facing them sit the kibbutzniks in khaki-colored work clothes, younger by many years than our hosts. We too have brought along our elder. His knowledge of Arabic does not extend much beyond the traditional greetings, which must be repeated several times to open a conversation, with long silences between each repetition. Our watchman is a member of our delegation. For ten years, ever since we came to settle here, he has been roaming our fields on horseback night and day and has learned to talk with the neighbors in their language. "When they swipe fruit, crops, irrigation pipes, that's a sign we're coexisting peacefully," he used to say. "It's only when the stealing stops and all is quiet that the signs point to a storm . . . ."

Another member of the party is our expert on Arabic matters. He has read many books about the people to which our neighbors belong and its history. He speaks their language with a literary accent and makes great efforts to understand them. He counts a great many Arabs among his friends.

Two worlds are meeting here. What we have in common is our hands, theirs like ours, with spatulate fingers, calloused from working the land; we both believe that there's enough land for both sides. In our hearts we are all fearful that war will break out between our two peoples. This is not the first time that, at our initiative, we are meeting. The first time our guys told the old men from the neighboring village, "For ten years we've been living together as good neighbors. Even when, at the beginning, we didn't always see eye to eye, in the end we could always find a way to agree. But now the day is coming when the land is going to be divided between Jews and Arabs, and bad things may happen, with consequences nobody can foresee. Let us come to an agreement, you and us: Whatever happens, no one will attack you, and no one will attack us . . . ."

This time we repeat this suggestion. An oppressive silence falls over the room. A piece of charcoal explodes in the stove. Sparks fly in all directions. The eyes of the fellahin are turned on their elder. All wait anxiously for him to speak.

"True. Our villages maintain good neighborly relations. There are no grounds for war between us, and with the help of Allah we will continue to live together in peace." Slowly he runs the back of his right hand over his silvery mustache to smooth it. "But what will happen"—he chooses each word with care—"when men mightier than you come to you in your kibbutz and attack us or when men who are greater and stronger than we come to us and attack you?"

A long silence. Our host remembers the coffee in the finjan and pours cupsful for everyone present. The conversation flickers back to life, like charcoal in a gust of air. We discuss many other matters, how we would go about meeting again in the hard times to come, but nothing can dispel the impression left by the elder's words, and the conversation dies out for good.

Much, much later our watchman shows me photographs he's secretly taken of the neighboring village, hidden among the low pines on the hillside above our kibbutz. An arrow points to the elder's house, another to the school situated on a slight rise at the center of the village. It was a square building of white limestone, where a young teacher from the city taught reading and writing to the children. He also led the older young people of the village, some of whom opposed us. Who knows how many of these young people are still alive and how many died?

The school bell rings shrilly. End of the school day. The shadowy halls of the high school are clamorous with the banging of doors and the sound of young voices. Once more I pass through the entrance hall with the marble tablets bearing the names of fallen students. Homer's nose is still smeared with India ink. I walk along a street of houses I recognize. People walk the other way, passing me. I see only shapes, not faces. A tram, with brand-new cars, runs past me. Distances have shrunk, but the square at the end of the street seems huge because the houses I remember around it have disappeared—all but one, the one I'm looking for. It rises in solitary splendor. Its denuded side walls still indicate where the neighboring houses stood before they collapsed in the hail of bombs. One of the buildings used to house the clothing store of the Weinberg family, my parents knew them.

"Who's there?" a woman's voice asks from behind the closed door. I tell her my name. The door opens a crack, just as far as the chain allows.

"What do you want?" the woman asks suspiciously. I repeat my name and remind her that I made an appointment with her that morning, by telephone.

"This morning? I don't remember." It is only when I tell her that my mother asked to be remembered that she grudgingly takes off the chain and opens the door.

Now I recognize her. In the dark hallway stands Frau Winkelmann, whose statement I am here to obtain. She looks exactly as she did before the Thousand Year Reich. She is small and slight, she is wearing a housecoat, just as she used to in the old days, always.

"And who might you be, young man?" She scrutinizes me with a searching look. Little bags droop below her glazed eyes, but the skin of her face is smooth, like that of a young woman.

I explain it all one more time. My mother, who lives in Israel, has sent me here to ask her, as a former friend of the family, to attest to whatever she knew about my family's holdings before they were expropriated. About the factory, for example. Hadn't she gotten my mother's letter? We talked about it on the phone less than an hour before.

"Factory, is that what you said? What kind of factory?"

"Cigarettes. C-i-g-a-r-e-t-t-e-s. Don't you remember?"

Blue veins stand out on the back of her tiny hand, which she places on her forehead. "You'll have to excuse me. My memory isn't what it used to be. I did send your mother a letter, a long time ago!"

I tell her we never received it.

"Are you sure? It must have gotten lost. Maybe I never sent it. Please, come in. If I wrote the letter and it never got there, it must still be here."

We enter a room thick with the smell of stale smoke. The windows are shut tight. They always were. The room always smelled of stale smoke, from Herr Winkelmann's pipe.

"It's too bad that my husband isn't here right now," she says. "Unfortunately he's passed on, but he visits me regularly. That's why I didn't change anything in the apartment." She points to the spines of books ranged on shelves along the walls and to the assortment of dozens of pipes of every shape and size, gathered on a round smoker's table. She turns back to me. "All right, now tell me, young man, to whom do I have the pleasure of speaking?"

With bad premonitions about the value of the statement I can expect to get here, I repeat my story. I remind her that when I was a little boy, I used to visit with my parents. I try to get her to understand that my mother needs proof in order to receive compensation for lost property.

"So your mother is still alive!" She arrives at this conclusion with absolute certainty. "And your father?"

I tell her that he died a few years ago.

"And your dear mother, how is she? What we went through here, you can't possibly imagine!" Now she is wide awake and speaks quite clearly. "Those terrible bombing raids. Night after night spent sitting in the cellar with all the neighbors."

I wonder if her Jewish neighbors, the Weinbergs, were part of the group in the cellar.

"My son-in-law fell at the front, and during one of the raids my daughter and her two children were buried under their house. My husband was lucky, he didn't have to go through any of that. I lost him early in the war. He's well and happy—at least that's some consolation to me."

What happened to the Weinbergs? I do not ask.

"Without my husband I couldn't have survived those terrible times. Imagine, first I had to let them operate on my kidneys, and then they took out half my stomach, and no sooner had I gotten over that surgery . . . ."

Her voice dies away, and I can only see her tiny moving lips. Herr Winkelmann is seated at the desk, behind a mountain of books, smoking his pipe. The bowl is ceramic, the stem a good eighteen inches long. Herr Winkelmann is wrapped in a blue dressing gown stitched all over with silver threads, and on his head he wears a red fez, which he claims to have brought back from one of his trips to Constantinople. A finger yellowed with nicotine points to the open newspaper, and he says to my father, "Gwendolyn. I've been watching that horse for months. Gwendolyn will win the next race for sure."

My father bets on Gwendolyn, just as he plays the state lottery every month. The day will come when he will get back the millions he lost during the inflation of the 1920s. Father stands at the edge of the racetrack, wearing a gray suit, his round, flat straw hat on his head. He is leaning on his stylish cane, black and thick, with a silver grip. His coat hangs open to reveal the glitter of a gold chain strung across his vest, at the end of which his gold watch is fastened.

He holds the watch under my nose. I say, "Snap." And the lid flies open and bumps my nose.

"Admit it," he replies to my mother. "How many non-Jewish friends do we have?" Mother has been complaining about the Winkelmanns' penny-pinching ways: though they offer us tea, they're visibly relieved when we politely decline. Father continues, "The Weinbergs next door aren't any better. Poor wretches. They talk about nothing but making money . . . ."

"The Winkelmanns aren't exactly rolling in dough either." Father's opinion cannot be changed.

"Maybe not rolling in it, but they have style. They never talk about money."

"Instead he brags about Constantinople. Turkey! I ask you! The man never even got close to the Turkish border! Maybe he read about it somewhere in his books. And she? She bores me to death with all her talk about her ailments." Father smiles. "You'll see that she'll out-live us all. A mended jug lasts forever."

"I always said that there's no end to the human ability to endure suffering . . . ." Now I can hear her voice again. "They've all left me. My daughter would still be alive, well and happy, if only she hadn't married that poor, unfortunate man. He was so determined to vol-unteer for the front. Everything around me is ruined. The neighbors are all gone . . . ."

Once more I refrain from asking what happened to the Weinberg family.

"I keep telling my husband that I've only one favor to ask of God, the Almighty: that he reunite us soon, so that we can be together for all eternity. Amen."

The smell of stale smoke in the unventilated room. I ask cautiously if she could please give me the statement she has prepared for my mother. Her eyes are staring at her husband's armchair. "What statement?" I see myself leaving empty-handed.

At this very moment she runs her hand over her forehead again. "Oh, dear God! I never offered you anything to drink! How could I be so forgetful? Please give my best to your mother, and tell her that she was smart to leave the country when she did. That way she was spared all the suffering that afflicted us. What we went through! But I'm sure I've composed a declaration for her. I discussed it with my husband. He thought very highly of your parents. Here." She takes an envelope from the desk and presses it into my hand. "What a good thing that your lost things will be restored to you. Nobody cares about us."

I say good-bye to my immortal hostess and go down the stairs. I never asked whether the Weinbergs were allowed to share the cellar during the bombing raids. But perhaps they were gone before then, deported to unknown parts, simply disappeared without anyone noticing.

"People don't just disappear. There are always eyewitnesses," we reassure each other. We are standing at the gate to the kibbutz waiting for Bernhard and Gabriel to return. As they do every morning, they've driven off early today to go to work—one of them to bake our bread in the ovens of the neighboring kibbutz, not quite three miles away on the other side of Abu-Sorek; the other to visit cowsheds in the neighborhood (he specializes in the artificial insemination of cows). It is a time laden with tension. A few months before, the United Nations passed the resolution that ordered the partition of the country and the establishment of a Jewish state. Gangs and lone wolves from among the local Arabs and those who infiltrated the country over the unguarded borders are shooting and killing Jews. Organized defense groups set out to retaliate. Mayhem all around, but we are still hopeful that a miracle will occur to calm things down. We never go to work in the fields anymore without carrying weapons and escorted by a guard. Only those who have urgent business travel to the nearby city. The bus windows are covered with iron grilles to protect the passengers against rocks and hand grenades. The Arab suburbs of the city can be crossed only in vehicles armored with plywood and sheet metal, pitiful protection against bullets.

We are still singing:

> The moon so pale in the sky,
> A far-off shout in the night,
> Sleep softly, dear valley,
> The watchers keep you in sight.

A civil war has broken out, waged by a number of different groups. One time in a residential section, another time on the highway; fire breaks out at one end of the country, dies down, and flares up again elsewhere. Arab legionnaires from the neighboring Kingdom of Jordan travel the roads in armored cars, machine guns mounted on top. Their presence does nothing to reinforce our sense of security, although they are under the command of a British general.

When the tension lets up even a little, Bernhard and Gabriel set off for work. Today, too, they have gone out, but this time they have not come back. Gabriel, driving home in his black car, picked up Bernhard in the neighboring kibbutz, and they haven't returned. Something that we do not dare imagine has happened to them on the road.

"People don't just disappear. There are always eyewitnesses." This is our way of giving each other courage, and we hope that our neighbors will keep to our agreement, even if it's one concluded only between us and never officially recognized. We did agree that neither place would do harm to the other. That's what we believed. As always in this kind of situation, the air is full of rumors, and there's no way of knowing where they originated. We had heard something about an incident on the road below Abu-Sorek; there are so many of these incidents these days. Somebody or other claims to have heard shots, but no one can say with certainty whether there really was gunfire or who was involved. According to others, the Arab Legion blocked off the road, took our comrades prisoner, and marched them off in an easterly direction. Our friends in charge of security for the kibbutz confer. If shots were actually fired, it is quite possible that they came from the revolver Gabriel carries to defend himself. The English police are alerted, but they show little inclination to look into the matter. We ask for help at the headquarters of the Haganah defense organization, where they have special sources of information. We also turn to our Arab neighbors to the west, the tenants of Kiri, and ask them to find out what happened on the road below Abu-Sorek. Although normally they have astonishingly effective ways and means of keeping informed about everything that happens for miles around, they tell us that they don't know a thing. Some of the young men—the same ones who came to us some time ago to help us in our work and secretly to train themselves for all eventualities—now take a drive below Abu-Sorek in a small pickup truck along the road where our friends disappeared. No one's in sight between the houses. By this time night is falling.

"In all probability they've been abducted," we tell ourselves to make ourselves feel better. In the kibbutz we are all despondent. Bernhard and Gabriel both have wives and little children. In the morning they drove to work, and in the evening they did not come back. We have to do something. We pass out our few guns to those who know how to use them. During the night we gather as a sort of emergency unit in the dark wooden dining hall. Silently we sit on the benches, lie on the tables. Bernhard and Gabriel. They must have been abducted. The neighbors saw and know all about it. The whole incident will turn out to be nothing more than a big misunderstanding. Everything will go back to how it was before.

Our men in charge of security confer without a break. Somebody proposes that we seize some of the Kiri tenant farmers as hostages. The proposal is rejected. The important thing is to avoid anything that will make the situation worse. Other possible plans are discussed, but gradually we become paralyzed by a feeling of helplessness. The suspicion gnaws at our hearts that everything is useless. We sit, as if in a trance, around the dark dining hall, hoping for the word that will free us from this terrible pressure, waiting for the deed that will wake us from the nightmare.

At dawn we go back to our rooms in the wooden barracks and the tents to rest for a few hours. During the days that follow we try to find out something, anything, from the people of Abu-Sorek. We are met with a wall of silence. Later someone deigns to tell us that on the day Bernhard and Gabriel disappeared, some people had arrived from elsewhere. What had they been doing on the road? Who knows. Even the village boys we ask shrug their shoulders. Their young teacher in his city suit calls them back sharply into the schoolroom. Nobody knows what he said to the village boys to explain what happened and how it came about.

How will my teacher explain to me what happened and why? I climb the creaking wooden stairs to the second floor and come to a stop at the door to his apartment. This was not a visit I had planned. A dull glass pane etched with vague floral designs is set into the upper part of the door. An oval enamel plate bears an inscription in Gothic lettering: Kober. I can hear a piano being played inside the apartment. One of the Bach suites. I wait patiently for the movement to come to an end before I pull the porcelain handle of the old-fashioned bell.

Nothing stirs. I pull on the bell again and listen to the approaching footsteps. A key creaks in the lock. The door opens. A man stands facing me, erect, dressed in a flawless gray suit just a tiny bit faded, a vest, a stiff collar, and a tie. It is Herr Kober, elementary-school teacher, subsequently music teacher at the high school. His hair has turned white, his little beard is gray. His head trembles and wobbles, the consequence of a disability incurred in the First World War. The glance from his blue eyes—I'd quite forgotten that they were blue— keeps me rooted to the spot. His stern expression takes me back at once to the schoolroom. We used to say, behind his back, that his head wobbled because he kept a metronome inside.

Heaven and earth
Must waste away,
But music, music
Will always stay.

"Yes?" he asks.

I introduce myself, I'd been one of his students for several years, and noting his surprised look, I add quickly that he probably wouldn't remember me; after all, hundreds of students had studied under his scepter. Oh, the thin, lithe cane he used to administer a beating to us, the quantity meted out with a sharp sense of justice!

Chance has brought me to the city, I explain, and I merely stopped by to say hello.

He cannot remember, but he says politely, "Come in, come in, sir!" He leads me along the hallway smelling of paste wax and into a room that is obviously the small apartment's parlor. There are a few old armchairs, white doilies on their armrests; the table with curved legs is also covered with a crocheted cloth, an empty crystal vase centered on it. On the walls hang colorful reproductions of pleasant landscapes and red-roofed houses clinging to mountainsides whose summits gleam in the rays of the setting sun. The room sparkles and shines with cleanliness. An old-fashioned piano stands in one corner; sheet music is open on the turned-back lid.

I say that I really don't want to interrupt his playing.

He replies politely, "It doesn't matter in the least. I've got time to spare. What does someone who's retired have to do? We kill time with a little tickling of the ivories . . . ."

What is this? He's home alone and plays the piano for his own edification, wearing a suit and tie?

"Yes?" he asks, eager to find out what I want with him. Once again I turn back into a schoolboy, and my voice falters as I explain who I am, where I come from, and when I was in his class. He still cannot recall. I add that he saved me from being expelled from high school when I had committed some unspeakable deed—all this, of course, in a time when no one could have any idea of the crimes that were later committed against the Jews.

"Ah," he exclaims, and his head trembles slightly, "that riffraff!" He snorts indignantly and repeats bitterly, "That riffraff!" With a broad gesture he invites me to sit down in one of the armchairs, and he himself sits facing me. I wait expectantly for what it is he has to say. Slowly I realize why I have come. My good old teacher will explain to me how and why what happened happened.

"D'you know what they did?" he asks, his voice thunderous. His blue eyes bore into mine, as always when he put a question in class.

"I know, I know," I mutter.

"You don't know a damn thing. You can't even begin to imagine!"
A flush spreads over his cheeks, and I remember that this used to be
a sign that any minute now his wrath would pour out over the delin-
quent student who did not do his homework. This time he stops himself, snorts a few times, and then, with barely contained rage, he
gasps, "Those bastards robbed me of my right to a pension. That's
right, they refused, those fine gentlemen. They simply refused to
promote me to the position of master teacher. That's how I lost my
rights!" He gestured at the shabby furniture. "That's what happens to
a teacher who served his country loyally for fifty-five years!" He goes
on and on about the wrongs he has suffered.

Just as I am beginning to ponder the best way to get out of there
quickly, he suddenly, without transition, asks about my family and
their well-being. I tell him that I live in a kibbutz. I have a vague
hope that life in a communal society might catch his interest, but no
such luck.

I ask about his wife. She was my first love—well, maybe the second. She was good-natured and invariably cheerful, a real child of
this town. Mother used to ask me, "Who do you love best?" And I
always answered, "Frau Kober. She's got a funny nose, blond hair,
and red cheeks. When I'm big, I'm going to marry her." The grown-
ups always laughed.

"My wife's gone shopping," he says, and I'm glad. This way I can
preserve her memory in my heart, young, cheerful, with cheeks of
velvet, like peaches.

Not far from my teacher's house is the street along the hillside—
the street with the house where I was born and spent my childhood.
The closer I get, the more convinced I am that I have come to the
right place. But I cannot recognize it. There is the intersection with
the grocery stores and the bakery where the soft pretzels—the ones I
like so much—are mounded in the window. It is the Sabbath, an
ordinary weekday for non-Jews. I enter the bakery's backyard and go
down the stairs into the room that holds the large oven set into the
white-tiled wall. The baker is shoving the black iron door upward,
and using the long-handled wooden paddle, he pulls a cast-iron two-
handled pan from the oven. It is the pan in which Mother has fixed a

cholent, in honor of the Sabbath, although there's nothing else we observe about the day of rest. I've brought along a towel so I can hold the hot handles.

"A Jewcake." The baker's boy laughs cozily and strews a handful of flour over the lump of dough lying on the table before him. "You got funny tastes, I've got to hand you that." He hits the lump of dough with the flat of his hand. A cloud of flour rises to the ceiling. He goes on kneading the dough with all his might.

"That pan has to be too heavy for you," the baker says, but I feel big and strong enough to carry the warm cake up the street that is as broad as an avenue and where our house is. The brown and crusty shell conceals a noodle pudding with raisins. My heart opens in anticipation of my favorite food.

My heart contracts with disappointment. The broad street of my childhood turns out to be more like an alley than an avenue. Instead of a multileveled, heavily laden beer wagon, drawn by husky Belgian horses who leave redolent droppings on the pavement, a municipal sanitation truck drives noisily by. Clattering metal and screeching brakes instead of sharp hoofbeats on cobblestones. But the church bells are still ringing.

Not far from the bakery an alley runs between two houses, leads to a small backyard that borders on a small garden. Elms and poplars grow in there. The street noises become distant, and if you listen carefully, you can make out the rustling of the leaves and the twittering of birds. The garden is bordered by a high fence. Children are not allowed. All the same, we squeeze through the fence, boys and girls, arrange ourselves in two rows, hold hands, and sing:

Open the gate,
Open the gate,
A golden coach is coming.

The first couple raise their hands to open the gate. One couple after another passes through. A prince drives up to look for a bride. The pure young voices rise to the heavens. Windows in all the houses around are thrown open. Mothers look kindly at their children's game down in the garden. The prince is still seeking his bride. Couples walk through the gate in time to the music, one more time and then one time more. Who will be the lucky couple? The girl with the skinny braids holding my hands urges me on so that we will get to the goal at the right moment.

Heaven or hell,
Ring out, wedding bells!

The gate closes. We are locked inside. The children shout happily, "Kiss her, kiss her!" Church bells ring. Some grown-up comes and drives us out of the garden.

Everything is narrow here, and small. I am the child, the world is large and hung with bells. I am the adult who has learned a thing or two about the true measurements of this world. I look across the street at my childhood home. The house is built of smooth, reddish stone. Its narrow entrance door is low, painted brown. Now it is white. Along the facade a bay window reaching up to the roof juts out from the second floor. The projection is held up by two sculpted female figures that grow out of the wall. Their brownstone breasts are, I remember, those of giantesses, but now they are rather small and modest. A childhood ditty comes to mind:

It was dark, the moon shone brightly
When a carriage rushing mightily
Slowly came around the corner . . . .

And suddenly I stand at the window on the fourth floor, behind the closed Venetian blind, peering out between the thin, green-enameled slats at my friends who are playing with aggies on the sidewalk across the street, on this very spot down here on the sidewalk. Tears fill my eyes. I swear that I'm never going to play with them again. They have stuck me with nicknames, half of which come from the realm of zoology; the other half always remain the same: "Jew!"

A few steps suffice to cross the street I remember as so wide, and I approach the door painted white and also brown. It is locked. Who lives in this house that sheltered my childhood? The bell pushes are yellow and worn. They are burnished and shiny, just like the whole new electric bell system through which you have to tell whoever asks who you are. What should I tell the slits in the metal plate? That I slid down the banister in the stairwell, although it was forbidden? That this was my little big world, which invited me each morning to make ever new discoveries?

On a summer morning I stand inside the door and open it, although it's hard for me to reach the knob. Outside, the sun is shining. On the sidewalk across the street my friends are rolling around with cheerful laughter. Like them, I throw myself on the pavement and squeal with joy. Then we play until Mother calls me to lunch. It is only after a long discussion, me on the street and she at the fourth-floor window, that I start for home. I'm afraid to go past the apartment on the ground floor. Behind the door a German shepherd lies in wait, big and lean like his master, who is called Arthur and of whom nobody in the world knows what he does for a living. Sometimes he beats up his wife, Claire. They have a son, too, shy and delicate, who answers to the name of Walter. They say his father is a Jew, a man his mother used to go with. Walter has a younger half-brother, Herbert, who was hit by a motorcycle and has had a limp ever since. Everything is Walter's fault, his parents say, and whenever Herbert does something terrible, it's Walter who gets the beating. When Arthur and Claire have a fight, she runs to my mother for comfort and support. A couple of hours later, the husband will climb the stairs to the fourth floor and beg his wife for another chance. Smiling happily, Claire will return to the ground-floor apartment in Arthur's muscular arms, and the two will get back to billing and cooing like turtledoves. Mother will say, "Riffraff . . . one minute they're tearing each other's eyes out, the next they're tearing their clothes off . . . ."

Herr Gutmann and his family live on the second floor. He's a converted Jew, he has been baptized a Lutheran; his hair has thinned out and he wears heavy, black horn-rimmed glasses. He looks like an intellectual, but he isn't. His pretty Christian wife used to work for his parents. The couple and their children celebrated Christmas with a stuffed goose under the tree hung with glittering balls and stars.

"Just don't ever bring a shikse home!" my mother warns, her voice threatening. "Not you and not your big sister. You're not allowed to marry non-Jews." If we do not understand why this is something we must not do, she is ready with the clincher: "If anything like that were to happen in our family, I'd kill myself."

I keep on going up the stairs. Sunbeams fall through the lead-bordered stained-glass windows of the landing between floors. On the third floor lives the very religious and very Catholic building superintendent with his wife, who always seems on the point of overflowing the limits of her clothes, and their two little girls whose names derive from the early Germanic period. Herr Bauernfreund cautions me for the very last time that ball playing is prohibited in the backyard. The yard abuts the place where the piano factory stores its shipping containers. I have found a secret hiding place among the crates, nobody else in the world knows about it. The shriek of the circular saw on the ground floor of the factory mingles wonderfully with the notes and chords elicited on the top floor, where the pianos are tuned. In the morning, at noon, and in the late afternoon the steamwhistle blows. After quitting time the smoke stops rising from the large redbrick chimney. I spend hour upon hour squatting in my huge crate, my school atlas on my knees, as I travel to faraway places.

Mother opens the door to me. "There you are! We were beginning to think you were lost and weren't ever going to come back!"

Above our apartment, on the fifth floor, Herr Pfleiderer, a saddler, and his family live in the attic, where there's a smell of paste wax and the ceilings slant. At Christmas my sister and I are invited to their apartment, and we admire the small, festively decorated tree, which stands over a small crèche the saddler whittled himself. A tiny, adorable baby Jesus lies in the manger. The Three Magi adore it. At Passover we take matzoth upstairs and explain to the saddler's son, who is the same age as my sister, the pictures in the Haggadah, the Hebrew text on one side and the German translation opposite. On holidays my mother usually sends presents upstairs for the saddler's son, who plays with my sister until one day he is big, wears a black uniform, and doesn't know us anymore.

We divide the people who live in the street into good neighbors and those from whom it's better to keep our distance. There is a clear distinction between decent and malicious non-Jews. These latter, in turn, are divided into those who are prey to a "healthy"—that is, tolerable—anti-Semitism and those who really hate Jews. Only the children forget, and they ignore the differences every time. They are at home everywhere, until one day the loudspeakers of the clunky radios pour out an unending torrent of shouts and martial music while silence spreads all around us, slowly and steadily. The poor kid on the ground floor, whose father is said to be Jewish, gets even more beatings than before. On the second floor no mention may be made of the fact that the head of the family has Jewish ancestors. There are still people who say, "They don't really mean it. They don't mean you, they're only talking about the Jews with money, the capitalists, the Bolsheviks. Those, sure; but not you . . . ."

But quickly the talk grows more cautious. The louder the noise, the wider grows the no-man's-land of silence surrounding us, which now goes with us wherever we go. More and more people take care not to enter it, as if it were sown with mines. Every well-meant expression toward us is discussed at length at the family dinner table, where we take our meals together—meals that grow more and more meager. My mother revives the custom of the Sabbath blessing, as it was done in the olden times. She sighs: "God is punishing us because we have forgotten the old customs. In times like these families must stick together." A simple world of rewards and punishments.

Our Jewish family doctor, whose face wore a good-natured smile whenever he made a house call, who lived alone with his old Christian housekeeper, commits suicide, and no one knows why. Maybe he was insulted to death because a Jew, in order to avoid any possible pollution of the German race, was not allowed to live under the same roof as a German woman. One day my mother lets out a terrible shriek when she is told on the phone that my favorite uncle, Uncle Siegfried, who ran a men's clothing store in a suburb of Duisburg, has been found dead in his home, together with Aunt Paula and with Margot, their daughter, whose eyes were always sad. They had turned on the gas because the German bookkeeper, who had lusted after my uncle's store, had denounced them to the tax authorities. My father spends hours on end lying on the couch and staring at the ceiling. Our factory is shut down because the city's cigarette dealers, each of whom my father knows personally, are afraid to distribute our cigarettes. In the corner, above the couch, hangs a wooden panel into which Mother, when she was young, had burned with red-hot needles:

Man needs a place,
No matter how small,
Of which he can say:
See, this is mine.

Here's where I love, here's where I live,
In sunshine or rain,
This is my home,
Here I'm at home.

I can hear Mother's voice: "You can't spend all day lying on the sofa brooding! Say something! You've got to do something, or do you expect us to beg for charity from the Jewish community?"

Father does not answer. In the evening he pokes around in the bookcase behind the books in their red bindings on which the names of German classics are inscribed in gold letters. He brings out the Hebrew Bible with all the glosses. He also finds a volume with extracts from the Cabala that he'd forgotten all about. He browses among the pages with their musty smell, searching for the meaning of the events that are descending on us. There are times, too, when he secretly goes out and visits the coffeehouse, where he plays cards with friends who, like him, are trying to forget their cares and miseries in the game. Mother stands at the window in her nightgown and waits until midnight for him to come home. Their quarreling voices wake me.

The rifts in the family deepen. One day my big sister leaves home. More and more often I seek refuge with my friends in the youth movement. There, in our clubhouse, there is still carefree joy, there is still hope. My family home collapses under the clamor of the new age, dissolves and ceases to exist.

The door is locked. There's nothing here for me anymore. I turn my back on the red-brick house in which my childhood is carved. Others have made it their own. There is no one here whom I could ask about the fate of those who used to live here. What happened to the baptized Jew from the second floor? Did his wife stick by him in the time of deportations? From whom could we demand accountability for the fate of the battered young boy on the ground floor whose father was said to be a Jew?

The well at the street corner where we could draw cool, clear water from a subterranean spring is no longer here. The three chestnut trees in the tiny park down the street have disappeared as well. In the spring they were strewn with glowing red and white flambeaux, and in the fall they cast a wealth of brown chestnuts. We made chains of them, which we hung around our necks.

Now all I want is to go back to the small hotel across from the synagogue, which stands at its old place and no longer stands. Perhaps they're holding a message for me, from the office that handles reparations: the woman who is working on my case has come to work. In that case I could go to see her this very day and leave town by evening. The thought of having to spend the night in this city, among the memorials of my past, bothers me no end. It's better not to spend the night alone with one's memories.

Two nights after Bernhard and Gabriel disappeared, the last Arab tenant farmers also vanished from Kiri. Apparently they were afraid that we would avenge ourselves on them for what happened to our comrades on the road below Abu-Sorek. Only a few families had remained in Kiri to the bitter end. They hoped to wangle more substantial compensation than they'd been offered for the land that belonged to us: land of their own and a stone house for each family on the other side of the valley, where their relatives had already moved. Perhaps they had other reasons as well for dragging out the negotiations. Rumor had it that people from outside were urging them not to enter into any agreement. Now they are gone. Nobody knows where. Perhaps they fled over the mountains toward the east. Perhaps they moved in with their relatives on the other side of the valley. The little village stands abandoned by people and animals. Some nights later we set out to tear down the last huts, where there is still the smell of smoke and manure. We take apart the tin roofs and the wooden beams that bore their weight. We topple the walls of rough stone. We don't feel comfortable at this work. No, it really isn't our fault that the last inhabitants of Kiri didn't have enough sense to resettle on the land of their own that was offered to them. And we did them no harm. We did not drive them out. We acquired the land legally. We bought it. Right is on our side. All the same, we have misgivings. We were refugees ourselves once, and now others are made homeless because they are foolish. We sense that what we are doing now is the beginning of something that will grow beyond our control. We take the beams and tin sheets down to the kibbutz. Soon we will be able to use them to shore up our defenses.

A Dream of New Beginnings

The hotel owner hands me a telephone message. Fräulein Hof-stetter, from the restitution office, is expecting me the following morning. Smiling weakly, the hotel owner adds, "I've been asked to take good care of you. As if we had to be asked. . . . We know perfectly well what our Jewish guests feel when they return to their old home."

Before he can be more specific about what it is that Jews feel when they come back here, I say, "Everything's fine. Thanks," and go up to my room.

In reality I am pretty depressed. It is two o'clock in the afternoon, and though I haven't eaten a thing since breakfast, I don't feel the slightest bit hungry. My little suitcase still lies on the bed unopened. What can I do until ten o'clock tomorrow? I go to the window and stare at the new synagogue, distempered a grayish white. I really should visit it, but something holds me back. I'm sure you have to ask for the key at the office, which is located in the long, low building next to the synagogue. It was burned down along with the school that was hastily set up in the rear courtyard when the Jewish children were expelled from the public schools.

In the yard they have staked out a little enclosed garden, where the congregation's sukkah stands. On Sukkoth, the harvest festival, the roof opens into two parts. We children stare in wonder at the branches and fruits that decorate the hut and still do not quite understand how you can sit outdoors in October, when it might start to rain at any moment. The rain grows visibly heavier. I open the window and breathe in the penetrating damp and chilly air. I stand and look.

"On Sukkoth you are to sit in the hut for seven days—that is what the Bible tells us," explains the rabbi who gives us religious instruction one afternoon a week, in the little classroom above the office across from the apartment of the non-Jewish custodian. The rabbi is a handsome man, dignified, with an awe-inspiring beard. He wears a frock coat cut in the latest fashion and looks more like a minister than a rabbi. We sit before him on narrow school benches and struggle to spell out the endlessly repeated prayer formulas that were going to bring us closer to the Incomprehensible. *You and Your exalted name . . . Yahwe, God of vengeance . . . He, Who knows all the secrets of the world . . . gracious and merciful Lord.* The God who, as a column of smoke, showed the children of Israel the way through the wilderness, and the angrily vengeful Father who can see into every corner of your heart, always demanding and punishing, who hurls fire onto the company of Korah or tears open the earth beneath it—that's someone I can imagine. That's a God you can sit down with, even if you're afraid of Him. It's hard to love Him, but you can rebel against Him. Not so the God Whom the rabbi represents as an idea the Jews have handed down to the rest of the world. How can a teenager love an idea that is not enveloped in thunder and lightning and clouds? One hour a week is reserved for reading selected Bible stories in German. The patriarchs Abraham, Isaac, and Jacob wander from place to place with their herds, which trail after them in long, orderly rows, like the ornate black letters in the reader. Every story, whether it is about kings or generals, has a moral, the consequences of crime and punishment, not at all like my beloved Greek and German myths. The rabbi teaches us bits of Jewish history as well. The Romans expelled the Jews from their country, such a long time ago that today the event has lost all meaning. Since then the Jews live in their own communities, spread all over the world, each community in the land it calls home. In the Dark Ages there were expulsions of Jews and pogroms, but we have long since come to live in an enlightened era; about a hundred and twenty years ago we were given the right to consider ourselves German citizens of the Hebrew faith. The rabbi seizes almost every occasion for mentioning the Jews who gave their lives for the Fatherland in the First World War.

"We celebrate the Feast of Sukkoth," he explains, "in remembrance of the Exodus from Egypt and the migration in the desert. Our forefathers were in a hurry, they could not build houses, and so they lived in huts and tents. There's another theory that says that in ancient Palestine Jews lived in huts during the time of the grape harvest so as to keep an eye on their vineyards." Boredom spreads through the class. Fortunately the girls are taught together with the boys. We could tease them, pull their pigtails, or send them insulting notes. We play our tricks openly and without shame. What do we care about the vineyards of the Jews in ancient Palestine, which is so distant from us? Thousands of years removed from us?

On a Sunday at the time of the grape harvest our family goes on an excursion to a village near the city. As far as the eye can see, vineyards extend down the slopes, all the way to the village, with its brown roofs and the little river running through the center. We sit in the hut outside the house of a vintner and drink his new wine. All around us other hikers sit on the rough-hewn benches, make a lot of noise, and sing at the top of their lungs:

I live in the mountains,
That is my home;
But down into the valleys
I love to roam.

We are all cheerful. My father takes pity on the wine left in the carafe. He pours himself another glass, though Mother warns him. He is not used to wine, she says, unlike the hikers next to us. He ignores her warnings. On the way to the trolley that will take us back to the city, however, he feels pretty lousy. Mother keeps an ostentatious silence, though from time to time she sighs half ironically, half provocatively. "Sure . . . sure . . . ." Which really means, "Nobody listened to me once again . . . as usual!" Father spits in annoyance. We children get a kick out of this dialogue.

At this moment I think for the first time since coming to this city this morning—I've lost all track of time—about my own family, my wife and our two sons. I see before me our little apartment in the watchtower at the edge of the kibbutz. The tower is on the east side, under the mountain ridge, on the other side of which live our Arab neighbors of Abu-Sorek. We built the watchtower in the first year of our settlement, after we had been shot at several times from the mountain in the night. The tower is three stories high. The top story consists of a parapet only, no windows, and is open like a hut. That is the place from which, at night, we watched the slope, which we lit up with a primitive searchlight to scare off anyone who might even be thinking of attacking us. That's also where we stood to flash messages in Morse code to the settlements on the other side of the valley—there were no telephones in those days. We planted a little vineyard on the slope behind the watchtower. It yielded only a few grapes, for the soil was meager and chalky.

The story below the platform served as a guardroom with narrow gun embrasures. Later we remodeled it into a living room for my young family. The ground floor was a kind of police station; ten guns were kept there, given to us by the British police so that we could protect ourselves from surprise attacks and other acts of violence. Once a week the British police sergeant turned up to check that we had not made any unauthorized use of the weaponry. In between his visits we practiced using the guns. One of us kept watch, the sergeant was not to take us by surprise.

Over there, on the other side of the low stone wall that marched down the mountain vertically, dividing the slope into two halves and marking the boundaries of our land, our neighbors in Abu-Sorek also planted a few vines. Even at a distance they looked pretty pathetic. Here and there they built primitive terraces of fieldstone, not like the vintners here do. What is the source of the rumor that vintners from around here drove into the city with horse carts and trucks to gather up the stones of the burned-out and collapsed synagogue and used them to terrace their vineyards? Did it happen in this city or elsewhere? I decide to drive out to the village where the owner of a particular vineyard lives. Perhaps he has the answer to my question.

"So what you're saying is you wanna go to work for me?" Herr Gerstenmaier lights one of his small cigars with rapt concentration, pulls the smoke into his lungs, and expels it with a look of deep enjoyment. Then he throws me a searching look from his clever eyes. "Lemme ask you—how old are you anyway?"

"Sixteen," I say, but I correct myself at once. "Almost sixteen."

"Hmm," he grunts and pours more cider into my glass and into that of my group leader, who is several years older.

That morning we had set out on our bicycles as we had done so often in years past, when we had gone out into the woods and fields on a Sunday with our buddies. In those days we wore Boy Scout uniforms, and at the head of our column we sported a pennant. We were also equipped with mess kits and military backpacks, to which we tied tents and sleeping bags. In all these things we imitated the German youth movement, where we had been undesirables for a long time now. Like them, we pitched our camp in unspoiled nature, we lit our campfires, we declaimed high-flown poems, and like them, we dreamed of a new kind of life in an unchanging community. We accompanied our songs with flutes and guitars. What we sang made up a strange hodgepodge of tunes. It's possible that future generations will not understand why we sang the songs of the mercenaries who devastated and plundered Europe during the Thirty Years' War:

> We set out so bold,
> Without baggage or gold,
> Tralala . . .

And at the same time we'd sing sentimental Yiddish songs of black-eyed girls and God-fearing Jews:

> As der rebbe Elimelech,
> Is gevordn zeyer freylech,
> Is gevordn zeyer freylich Elimelech,
> Hot er oysgetun den kittl,
> Un hot angetun die hittl
> Un geshikt noch die fiddler die zvey . . . .

Today people will be amazed that we loved the German songs with all our hearts, the songs that resounded with yearning and admiration for the marvelous landscape of home:

> No land more beautiful in this our history
> Than this our land as far as eye can see.

But we also sang songs from faraway Palestine, in Hebrew, and these also touched a romantic chord in us, although most of us could not quite understand the words we were singing:

Al ss'fat yam kineret . . .
[On the shores of the Kineret
Stands a splendid palace,
God's garden is planted there . . .]

"Of the vultures' black flock" was a song from the Peasants' War, and then there were songs of the revolutionary workers:

On the barricades,
You courageous workers . . . .

And Budenny's bold horsemen galloped out of the Russian Revolution into our songs. Only gradually did we enlarge our repertoire with the songs of despair and protest that spoke of the political turmoil and the economic hardships of the 1920s:

Come on out from those dank holes.
They say those are your homes . . . .

Reality was too depressing for young men to challenge without a dream. We were young, and we felt entitled to participate in every world there was. Whatever slogans agreed with our joyous sense of life we inscribed on our pennants, even if some things did not really fit with some of the other things.

We were wild about the aristocratic attitude demonstrated to us in the neo-Romantic poetry of a Stefan George. At the same time we poured over the Hasidic tales of the humble Rabbi Sussya of Tarnopol and the mysterious Rabbi Nachman of Brazlav and other Hasidic mystics. Influenced by Gustav Landauer, we looked for our own path toward the realization of a humane socialism, always aware of the failure of the German Social Democratic Party and the excesses of the Bolshevik revolution. We wanted to give meaning to the fact that we were born Jews, without knowing where it would lead us. We began to learn Hebrew and to study modern biblical exegesis. We were filled with the belief that the community was the means to free the individual from the alienation of man from man, of man from the All. We dared to hope that the realization of all the things we believed in would lend meaning and substance to our lives. "The community is the Mount Sinai of the future": we repeated the words of Martin Buber with almost religious fervor. A common element in the statements of all those in whose footsteps we were treading was the profound, aphoristic, sometimes quite obscure, form of expression, at a time when the German language was also fraught with irrationality. But in this way we could identify with the profundity of the words without having to define the meaning precisely.

If it had been possible for us to realize our plan and establish a commune in Germany, we would probably have failed, like others who try it today, a generation later. It has to be said in our defense that in spite of the jumble in our heads we were able to understand the signs of the times and to choose a road closer to reality—the establishment of a kibbutz commune in Israel. But the debate between utopia and what is called reality goes on, openly or covertly, consciously or unconsciously. In the course of time the youthful enchantment that clung to the idealistic pursuit of the unattainable faded. But it was granted to us to build an actual little world, here on this earth.

"Almost sixteen . . . ." Herr Gerstenmaier shakes his head with some misgivings. "And you're serious about wanting to work in my truck garden? In your whole life, have you ever worked—I mean, with your hands?"

I summon up all my courage. "Maybe I'm not all that tall, but I'm really very athletic."

My friend adds, "We want to emigrate to Palestine, all of us together."

"Ah," the gardener says, and he gazes thoughtfully at the ash that grows longer and longer at the tip of his cigar. "So that's what it's all about. I personally got nothing against Jews, not a thing. You could even say the opposite's true. Before I married her, the wife worked for a Jewish family in the city. Oppenheimer. Oppenheimer's shoe store. You know them?" Before we can reply, he says emphatically, "Good folks. They treated my Emma like she was their own daughter. . . ." Once again his searching look scrutinizes me. "So let's wait for the wife, see what she's got to say. And while we're waiting, how about we have something to eat?" From the kitchen cupboard he takes a loaf of rye bread, butter, and a fragrant piece of cheese and sets them down on the table. He adds plates and eating utensils.

"Wait while I get us a fresh radish from the garden. A meal without a radish isn't a meal at all." He leaves the room, which is both the family's kitchen and its living room; it is in a kind of half-basement, and we watch him through the window as he goes up the stairs. We look around the plain kitchen. On the wall, beside the white cupboard, hangs a square porcelain kitchen clock; it's five minutes slow. In the other corner stands a broad woodstove; the family dinner is cooking in several pots. It smells of cabbage and pot roast. Beside the stove, near the sink of reddish terrazzo, stands a wooden sideboard, pans and cooking utensils hang from the wall over it. We sit on the other side, at the big table in the comfortable dinette. Through the window behind us, at the level of the path outside, you can see beds of vegetables and flowers, as well as some that are encased in low wooden boxes and covered with glassed-over metal frames. Some of these frames are ajar, held open by little wooden dowels. Behind the beds an open field, a low, tree-covered hill. Herr Gerstenmaier comes back with two huge, moistly glistening radishes. The water he used to rinse the dirt off them is still running off, and he throws them on the table.

"Okay, gentlemen, let's hop to it . . . !" He pulls a heavy gardener's knife from his pants pocket, snaps open a blade whose tip is rounded in a half-moon shape, and expertly cuts the radish—miraculously it holds its shape—into a kind of accordion of thin slices.

"Pick up your knife, kid, don't be shy," he turns to me. "First test in the gardening trade: the art of cutting a radish so that the juice runs out." He gives a sensuous laugh. I look with awed astonishment at the stocky man who in honor of Sunday is wearing a white shirt without a collar and black trousers held up by suspenders. His hands are strong, the skin on them is cracked, and his nails are rimmed in black. A round peasant's head sits on his broad shoulders. It is covered with short, curly hair. He has a little mustache as well, and shrewdness gleams in his narrowed eyes. When he becomes aware of my pitiful attempts to slice the radish, he asks with a hint of mockery, "And your mom and dad, young man, what do they have to say about this? Don't they want you to be a lawyer or sumpin' like that?" He bursts into loud, good-natured laughter, and suddenly he resembles a billy goat. My friend explains enthusiastically that the time has come for Jews to work with their hands again. He also confides that we want to rebuild our country with our own hands, and more along the same lines.

> Work, work is our entire life,
> Work will lift us above want and strife.

That, too, was one of our songs in those days.

Herr Gerstenmaier listens attentively, now and again grunting as a sign of approval. It is not clear whether we have been able to convince him altogether. In the meantime he has finished cutting his radish, placed it on his plate upright, the tail end on top, and presses it hard until the juice runs down the slices. Then he blinks merrily at me: "Look . . . that's how it's done. A radish is like a person. You got to squeeze him properly to get the best out of him. . . . Why ain't you eating? Dig in! You got to be strong to work. Nothin' comes from nothin'. That's what they say. And they say: If you know what work's all about / And you don't choose to be lazy, / Then, man, you're plumb crazy. And you don't know what work is, and you want to try it. Our helper ran off a coupla days ago. All right, we could work sumpin' out . . . ."

Once again he gives me that sidelong look, as if his eyes wanted to explore my arms to test whether my muscles are tough enough. The unaccustomed cider is muddling my senses, but all the same, the fact that he might actually risk accepting me to work for him penetrates my brain. I'm overcome with sudden fear. Can I explain to my parents that I want to become a simple workman? How do I explain to this man here that these days parents no longer have a say?

Actually I wanted to ride the local train one more time; running on narrow-gauge rails, it used to connect the village with the city, jerking from station to station. But I am told that the service was discontinued some years ago. The bus in which I'm traveling is riding through the outskirts. Across from me sit two high-school students, both of them blond, apparently on their way home from school. One of them is holding a slim book, from which he is enthusiastically reading a poem to his buddy. Schiller? Hölderlin? Hard to say; in any case, an elevated style. The sight of two village youths reading poetry warms the cockles of my heart.

"Big words don't mean a thing to me. I'm an old, plain Social Democrat," says the gardener. "I can tell you guys the truth. This is what it is: As I see it, Jews are people just like anybody else. They can all go to hell."

I assume he means the other villagers. Just maybe he really does mean "all."

"I figure right now they're giving the Jews a hard time. That's no reason to give up. You're still young. Okay, go ahead, dig in."

I look at the slab of black bread and butter in my hand. The bite I've taken sticks in my throat. The gardener is like the woman who pushes her way into Oppenheimer's shoe store in the main street, swearing all the time, paying no attention to the shouted abuse of the men in brown shirts who block the entrance. They hold up signs reading, "Germans! Do not buy from Jews!" and "The Jews are our misfortune!"

I stand on the opposite side of the street, in my short pants, and I feel a space hollowing out in my heart. And like a tidal wave, something unfamiliar sweeps in to fill that emptiness, carrying me along. "A Jew—that's me! Events they say happened in the past and won't ever happen again—they're talking about me!" A certainty rises from the vacuum in my heart: "They can put me outside the law. Anybody, if he feels like it, can shoot me down like a duck. Hunting season all year round. I'm the one they can deprive of the right to live in this world. Me, and all the other Jews."

The boy sitting across from me has finished his recitation, and both of the students look out the window at the passing fields. It is their country, their home. No one would think of contesting that fact, even if their country is still occupied by foreign soldiers. Even after a lost war they are safe.

Once again I hear someone say, "Under no circumstances must we allow this land to revert to lawlessness." A week has passed since Bernhard and Gabriel's disappearance. The last remaining tenants of Kiri have run off, and the inhabitants of Abu-Sorek have stopped speaking to us. The air is thick with rumors. Anybody who has any kind of relations with Arabs has an informant, from whom he gets whatever news there is. In this way we hear completely conflicting versions of what happened. It is said that a group of Arabs had come from far away, erected a barricade on the road, and abducted our

friends in their car, perhaps for purposes of extortion. Others object
that whatever took place so near Abu-Sorek could not have happened
without the knowledge and complicity of the villagers, who have
always been known for their pride and willfulness. There was no way
that any bandit from who knows where could do whatever he wanted in their territory. That's what they said . . . .

One day we are given the news that the abducted car has been
sighted in the capital city of a neighboring state. We think that now
it's all right to hope that regular soldiers of that state were involved in
the incident rather than a common gang. Could our friends be the
first prisoners in this war that has not even been declared yet? One
more day passes, then another. In our hearts the suspicion that Bernhard and Gabriel have been murdered grows into a certainty.

One evening, under cover of darkness, so that the British military
and police will not notice, dozens of men, singly and in groups, arrive
at our kibbutz. They have come from settlements on the other side of
the valley. They come in their work clothes; each one is armed. Our
men are not supposed to take part in the action planned against our
neighbors of Abu-Sorek, who are being held responsible for active, or
at least passive, participation in the offense against our friends. After
all, we are going to have to go on living with our neighbors. That is
why we are assigned the task of keeping watch on our kibbutz by ringing it with sentries. Anyone who does not have a gun holds a club.
Darkness descends on the kibbutz. In the wooden huts and in the
tents, in the first cement houses we have built in the course of the
eleven years since we came here, all the lights are dimmed. Another
night of tense nerves, like so many others. But this night is different
from all others. This time something that has never happened before
will occur. Somewhere or other it has been decided that there must
be a show of strength, that a surprise blow must be struck, that someone must be taught a lesson. Nobody knows whether this will bring
our friends back, but not to respond at all—that seems intolerable.
That is what everyone is saying. It doesn't occur to anybody that this
step will be the first link in an unending chain of action and reaction.

Shortly before midnight the men from the other side of the valley
move outside the fence and take up their positions facing the neighboring village. An hour passes, and then another. Dull and sticky tension lies over the kibbutz. Suddenly two gunshots ring out, followed

closely by another. From the direction of the communal kitchen, a cement building with gun embrasures designated the command post for this night, excited voices can be heard. A little later, before dawn, all the groups return to the kibbutz without having accomplished a thing. The shots all came from the neighbors. In all probability they got wind that something was up. It is explained to us that the element of surprise has been lost, that it would make little sense to go on. The armed men, farmers like ourselves, go back home to their work early in the morning. A few nights later a small Arab village is shelled in a surprise attack. It lies a few kilometers farther to the east. The shelled village probably had little or nothing to do with Bernhard and Gabriel's disappearance near Abu-Sorek. We try to understand what is behind the incidents in our part of the world, which now go far beyond neighborhood conflicts. Jewish and Arab settlements run all along the road that connects the hamlets of the interior with Haifa, the seaport on the Mediterranean. Day by day it becomes more dangerous to drive through an Arab village. The inhabitants throw stones, shoot, throw hand grenades. The Arab Legion, the military arm of the Kingdom of Jordan, still patrols the road in its armored cars, steel vehicles with turrets where soldiers wearing red-and-white-checkered kaffiyehs squat behind machine guns. This is the way we are inextricably linked, and no one can say with certainty who is more afraid of his neighbors.

They also say that everything that happens on this road is just the beginning of the struggle for an opening to the sea. In all the Jewish settlements they are digging trenches. The day is approaching when the land is to be partitioned and the Jewish state established. Tensions mount from day to day.

The bus drives through the main street into the peaceful village. The two students get out with me at the town center and go on their way. Across the street stands the White Stag Inn. The sign is new. Gerstenmaier used to meet his cronies here once a week for a game of cards.

Around midnight, a little bit drunk, they would start out for home, shaking the windowpanes with their singing:

Bunnies graze upon the meadow,
And in the water swim the fish.

I'd rather have no girl at all
Than this cheatin', lyin' dish.

On the hill across from the inn stands the church with the square bell tower, and next to it the three-story town hall with a sundial over the entrance, both unchanged. The street that leads to Gerstenmaier's house at the end of the village has been paved.

I see myself pulling a handcart, in it a basket full of fragrant rye bread that Frau Gerstenmaier baked in the communal oven. I must take care that the cart does not overturn in one of the deep ruts the wheels of the farmers' carts have dug into the loess or, worse yet, that the cart does not fall into one of the potholes full of rainwater.

Now asphalt covers the wagon traces and potholes. The houses with their gabled roofs look clean and cared for. Here and there a second story has been added. The wooden fences along the street are painted, not a picket is missing. Tractors stand in the yards, here and there a high-racked wagon. Outside some of the houses there are manure heaps, neat and precise, as if they had been drawn with a ruler. I recognize the farms of Karl and Franz, the gardener's friends. Karl came with his horses to plow Gerstenmaier's fields every time. Franz, a bachelor, was renowned in the village for chasing girls and getting into fights. I can still see the fearsome mustache he wore to advertise his virility. Two farm women are absorbed in a cozy chat in front of one house. They acknowledge my greeting with a slight nod: "Mornin'." Their eyes follow me as I pass them with my bread-laden cart. I can feel their prying gaze, their curiosity about the Jewboy from the city who works in Gerstenmaier's gardens.

People dressed in city clothes come in the opposite direction and pass me. No one says hello or nods. This is the village where I almost became a man. This is not that village.

The gardener's house is washed in pink. It has three stories, and on the top floor there is an attic room where the ceiling slants—my room. The window is set in a dormer, at the center of the tiled roof, with a view of the garden. We are standing next to the shed built on to the house, where twice a week the vegetables are prepared for market in the city.

We are waiting for Frau Gerstenmaier to come back from church at long last. She is skinny, with an upright bearing, she has a long nose, and her right hand, with which she holds her prayer book, is missing a finger. She wanted to speak with my parents, as was only proper, before she would agree to any arrangement. It's easy to tell that she is not overly enthusiastic about hiring me of all people. As she stands there before us, gaunt and stiff, holding the prayer book, the impression she makes a very different impression from that of her good-natured and easygoing husband.

Sometimes, as a way of teasing her, he would run his hand across her flat chest in front of everyone and announce loudly, "Nothin', absolutely nothin'. Like a scarecrow!"

Their children—five-year-old blond Herbert, and Margot, two years younger and with her father's brown curls—welcome me enthusiastically, especially when they discover that I can tell stories.

My mother is beside herself. "My son nothing more than a farmer's helper? We haven't sunk so low yet!" Father remains silent. In the end they give in. Mother goes out to the village to check whether the Gerstenmaier family is worthy of teaching her son the art of truck farming. She comes home satisfied.

On the agreed-upon day I arrive at the flower and vegetable market outside the city hall to move to my new home with Frau Gerstenmaier. It is close to noon. All around, baskets and boxes are being loaded onto trucks. I place myself and my suitcase near the stand where the gardener's wife has been selling lettuce and radishes, tomatoes and parsley since early morning. The place smells of wet leaves. The early-summer sun shines on the noisy commotion that goes along with dismantling the booths. "Go ahead, help the driver load up," Frau Gerstenmaier says as she continues to count her day's earnings in the leather satchel at her waist. Hesitantly I put my suitcase down on the cobblestones and obediently hand empty baskets up to the driver. What would my schoolmates say if they could see me now as I deal with my new chore? And besides: How am I supposed to go with her? How many seats are there in the cab? The gardener's wife, as if guessing my thoughts, announces tersely, "Climb in, we're off." Clutching the suitcase my mother packed this morning, choking back her tears, I clamber over the wooden rail and find a place to sit between the baskets and the remnants of unsold vegetables. Enormous embarrassment overwhelms me. It is one thing to decide that I want to become a farmer; it is far less simple when you are no longer treated like the scion of a nice, middle-class family but have become just another farmhand.

This is the beginning of a hard time for me. It is as if I had fallen into a bottomless pit. From early morning to late at night there is hoeing, digging, watering two beds at one time with heavy watering cans, carting out manure and pumping sewage, planting seedlings, weeding, picking vegetables, hauling heavy baskets, washing and sorting vegetables—hours on end, like every member of the gardener's family. It starts at sunrise. "You up there . . . don't go by the kitchen clock to get up. It's always slow!" the gardener calls as he tosses a pebble up at my dormer window. I wash my face at the tap in the garden, where I have stumbled in a sleepy stupor. I struggle with exhaustion until night, when I fall asleep over the textbook from which I try to teach myself Hebrew. The skin of my hands is torn to ribbons. The wounds get infected. Every muscle in my body hurts. There is room in my head for only one thought: Don't give up. Prove to them that you can do it! Carry on, under the burning sun or in the rain that turns the paths to mud, the gardener's voice and cackling laughter at my back. He urges me on, he encourages me, he scolds me and with infinite patience explains how to hold a hoe or a spade, how to plant and prune. In between, he curses the new government or, with an amused smile, tells stories of his romantic conquests when he'd been young and free, before he'd been trapped in the net of a wife. When a field of cauliflower or tomatoes is to be hoed or weeded, or when vegetables have to be picked for market, we have help from the wife's mother and father, who are retired to the part of the property reserved for the old folks, behind the little woods, on the hill above the edge of the farm. There, between the fir trees, near an abandoned quarry, stands their little house. Gerstenmaier's greenhouse, where he raises early tomatoes and dahlias, is located nearby. Klara, Frau Gerstenmaier's sister, a girl born late in her parents' lives, also lives with them. She, too, helps with the work sometimes. She is not much older than I am. She wears her hair in a lustrous auburn braid, long and thick. Klara is no beauty. Her nose is long, like her sister's; she is sturdily built, with broad hips, and her breasts are those of a grown woman. When they drive by the truck garden on their way to the fields, the farmers atop their wagons check out her figure with experienced eyes and undisguised admiration. They miss no opportunity for a suggestive remark whenever they see Klara bent over a bed, when she is plucking gooseberries or apples in Gerstenmaier's vineyard, on the other side of the road. The vineyard is terraced, the levels supported by roughly trimmed stones. It's a little bit neglected, the vineyard. It's my favorite place. You can hide behind the bushes or rest in the shade of the apple trees without anyone's noticing. In time the vineyard becomes the meeting place for some friends from our movement; at my gardener's instigation, they have found work with farmers from the village. Among them is a young girl from the city; her dark beauty causes restlessness among the village boys and envy in the women and girls. So Gerstenmaier informed us. Now and again, after a brutal summer workday, we meet in the vineyard and report to each other about what we are encountering in this experiment, how we are managing to grow accustomed to village life. The news of events in the rest of the country and of everything that is happening to the Jews reaches us as if through a fog. Most of the time we are too tired to really understand and interpret what we have heard. In these nights we dream of the day when we will leave here and return to the country that is ours to establish a new society and to live in communal peace.

> We came to the land,
> We came to the land,
> We plowed the earth,
> We sowed the seeds,
> We wait for the harvest still . . . .

Only when I visit the city from the seemingly quiet village do I sense the terrible turmoil that is hurtling the Jews hither and yon. On the eve of Yom Kippur I rush home to go to the synagogue with my parents. It is not prayer that I need but the community. I am certain that the persecutions have aroused a sense of solidarity among the Jews. Those affected by a common fate would unite in a genuine community. The long-forgotten history of one people would be given new meaning.

When I arrive at my parents' house, they have already gone on ahead. I do not get to the synagogue until after the start of the service. Some of the congregation's dignitaries are standing beside the entrance. Dressed in black suits and top hats, they talk with each other in hushed voices, their eyes darting all around restlessly, mistrustfully. The synagogue is crammed. With difficulty I find a seat in the last row. At a distance I catch sight of my father, bent over his prayer book. The cantor sings and the congregation replies, each in its own rhythm. I look around, searching the expressionless faces for a spark of emotion. "Thou art holy, and awesome is thy name. There is no God but thou." Upstairs, in the gallery, the mothers and other women sit enthroned in festive dress, as they have sat since time immemorial.

"And forgive us our trespasses . . . ." Between prayers the men around me whisper about the political situation and economic conditions.

"We have failed . . . betrayed . . . broken promises . . . stolen . . . given false testimony . . . ."

The cantor blows the shofar. Its piercing tone could break your heart. Soon those wanderers in the wilderness will rise, one people, one with itself and its history. I look around me and listen to the soft murmur that replies to the cantor. Not a shout to pierce the heavens. I have fallen prey to an illusion. Where is God hiding Himself?

I am still standing at the back of the gardener's house. The sky is heavy with rain clouds. Not a soul can be seen in the bare and abandoned beds. Not much has changed here, only the vineyard with its fruit trees is gone. Now carefully maintained houses, set off by low stone walls, have taken its place.

In the fall we pick apples in the vineyard and put them through a wooden press until the thick, brown juice runs into the tub. Later it will be brewed into cider to last all year long. I have become used to the work. My arm muscles have grown hard, my hands are broad and powerful. Now I raise my eyes from the soil, and they discover the sky once more. Life could have been sweet if only the threat had not always hung over us. One day our friend, the young, dark-haired girl, leaves the village hastily. Gerstenmaier reports with relish what people are saying. The farmer she worked for is said to have tried to get into her room at night. According to another rumor, a young farmer became overly importunate while she was working in the fields alone.

That is the version told by Karl and Franz, who don't bother to hide the fact that they were just as eager to claim the virginity of a good-looking, big-busted Jewish girl.

"But hey, they're all the same," the gardener laughs. "One's got a little more, another less . . . ." At a distance his hand strokes his wife's bosom. Everyone understands that they're not all the same.

One day Karl brings the gardener a newborn fawn he has found in the fields. The fawn leaps and gambols in the shed. Margot and Herbert, the children, play with him. The next day the gardener pulls the fawn over to the runoff and pulls out the gardening knife with the sickle-shaped blade. The fawn cries piteously until the blood flows into the runoff from its slashed throat. Deeply shaken, I follow the proceedings. For the first time in my life I see how killing is done. The meat is destined for the Sunday roast, when I will be in the city.

I walk around the shed, go down the stairs to the basement level, and ring the bell. A young woman comes to the door. I ask for Herr Gerstenmaier.

"Which one?" she wants to know.

"Ernst Gerstenmaier."

"He doesn't live here anymore. He's over that way now." She points in the direction of the hill with the copse and the abandoned quarry.

I say, surprised, "The old folks' section! He can't be that old!"

The young woman grows a little suspicious. "May I ask to whom I'm speaking?"

I tell her that I knew the gardener many years ago and that I have now come from Israel to ask him a question.

"Oh, then you're the Jewish guy who used to work here a long time ago! I'm the daughter-in-law, I'm married to Herbert. You told stories to him and his sister, Margot." She gives me a friendly smile. "Come in a minute, come in, come in. You're part of the family history, after all."

In the kitchen there is new furniture, an electric stove, a refrigerator. The clock that was always five minutes slow is gone.

"Can I get you something? I can make a pot of coffee. Herbert's gone to town; he'll be back in an hour."

I want to see my gardener, but first I have to have coffee with the daughter-in-law.

"You can go over there right after," she reassures me. She explains that she and Herbert have taken over the farm while Margot, her sister-in-law, is married to a boilermaker who works in the city. Smiling good-naturedly, she says, "Margot's husband almost made it all the way over there, to you people in Palestine. He was a soldier with Rommel . . . ."

In the mountains above the kibbutz, between the pines we planted, English soldiers dig ditches and cannon emplacements for what may be a further retreat for them and the final battle for us.

"Lucky for me he didn't make it," I say quietly, returning her smile.

"But why?" she asks, completely innocent.

"Because that would have been the end of us."

Skeptical, she replies, "Is that really true . . . ?" She does not understand any of it, and I don't care. I want to go see my gardener.

"I'll call him and tell him you're coming." Now they have telephones. In my day we shouted from one end of the farm to the other if we had something to say to each other.

***

A Building Site for Refugees

"You know the way," she calls at my back as I climb up the outside stairs.

I turn around. "How is Klara?" I ask with some hesitation.

Her face becomes closed off, as if a curtain had been drawn across it. "You'd better ask the old folks. They'll tell you all about it."

So I go up the path. Between the truck garden and the vineyard. I see the apple trees and the bushes, some with little red berries, others sporting larger ones, with a thicker, hairy skin. They are distributed across the narrow terraces connected by clumsy steps, these too made of crude, barely hewn stones. Splendid ornamental shrubs edge the steps, which are covered with polished marble slabs and lead to an artfully wrought iron gate. The gate is set between walls made of square-cut stones between which here and there large square ashlars stick out, giving the wall an artificially fancy character. Behind the walls are the new buildings, these too surrounded by exotic ornamental trees. Klara stands barefoot on the ladder hammered together of coarse wood and picks apples. Her sturdy legs are sunburned. She calls out to me to take the full basket from her. On the other side of the path the glass panes that cover the beds glitter in the sunlight. We carefully pluck tiny seedlings from a bed framed in wooden boards. The young plants have grown from seeds we dropped in the black soil on cold winter days. We prepared the germinating beds early in the winter, in the bitter cold: first a layer of dust and soil, sifted out from the city's wastes, topped by a layer of horse manure warm enough to be steaming, brought straight from the stables of the nearby garrison. The dung is supposed to supply warmth to the seeds germinating in the top layer of good soil.

Now spring is approaching, though winter is not quite gone. An icy wind paralyzes our fingers. Klara crouches across from me, bent

over the boxed-in bed, and deftly pulls out the closely ranked seedlings, which we will replant at once in another bed, with more space
between them so that they have room to flourish. In spite of the cold,
she has not buttoned her jacket. I can see her firm breasts at the neckline of her plain blouse. She turns up rather frequently to help me as
I work. Her proximity confuses me. We don't have a whole lot to say
to each other.

"Of course I'm not as smart as your Jewish girls in the city, the
ones you go to every other Sunday . . . ," she says after a long silence,
and she leaves. The farmers drive by on their wagons, muffled in
their jackets. They look at us and say not a word. They do not even
let one of their usual jokes pass their lips.

It is growing dark. A large rock, still slightly moist from the rain,
lies at the side of the path. I sit down.

"Your Jewboy's grown into a real man," Franz announces one
night. He and Karl have come to discuss something with the gardener. Franz sports a bandage over his left eye.

"A pirate—that's what you look like," Gerstenmaier banters.
"Couldn't stay away from a fight, could you?" They sit around the
kitchen table for a good long while and discuss every detail of the fra-
cas that broke out at the White Stag Inn two days earlier. The fight
was between local guys and a gang from the neighboring village. As
Franz tells it, the men from the other village had taken too much of
an interest in the girls from our own. The three crack jokes and drink
the wine the gardener has brought up from the cellar. An abundance
of apples fill cellar shelves above the barrels of cider and wine. The
fragrance of apples fills the entire house. Frau Gerstenmaier is also
sitting at the table, mending sheets. She is the first to understand
that the two farmers have not come to talk about the free-for-all in
the village tavern. She suggests that I go to bed. Fairly reluctantly I
leave the warm kitchen and climb up to my cold little room under
the eaves. Surprising us all, winter is paying a return visit. A thin
blanket of snow covers the ground. On the floor below, outside the
Gerstenmaiers' bedroom, I stop and, standing in the dark corridor,
listen to the hushed voices rising from below. I cannot make out
clearly what they are talking about until Frau Gerstenmaier's sharp
voice carries up the staircase.

"He's a good kid . . . he was just a boy when he started. Couldn't even hold a pitchfork. And now he works like a real man."

"Sure. Could be that it pays to have him around. But somebody like him on the farm"—the voice is Karl's—"I can't say I'm sure that in the long run it'll pay off, Ernst."

Gerstenmaier is all bluster. "First you all laughed at me for wanting to train somebody like him, a good-for-nothing. And now you're saying that I'm lookin' to make a profit. Just for your information: The moment he's learned to do the work properly, he gets his wages—that's only right and proper."

Now they all speak at once. I tiptoe down the stairs so as to hear better. A step creaks. The voices stop. The kitchen door opens. The gardener's wife steps out and remains standing in the beam of light that comes from the kitchen. She turns her face upward, up the stairs. "Thought I heard sumpin' . . . like the kids woke up."

The gardener's voice: "Leave the door open."

She goes back into the kitchen without closing the door completely. The discussion continues. This time the speaker is Karl. "You really oughta care, Ernst, about what people are saying."

"There's a lot of talk when the day is long," the gardener says; his voice is full of contempt. "After all, I'm not the only one in the village that's got a Jewboy working for him. If the wife would agree, I'd jump at the chance to hire one of those Jewgirls, too, like the one that ran off. She could learn all kinds of stuff here, ain't that the truth?" He chuckles cheerfully. "But what can I tell you? The wife won't have it."

"Don't listen to the old goat," his wife says. Her voice is tinged with worry.

"You're lucky that only your friends can hear your blather," Franz grumbles.

"So let's drink to your eye that they almost knocked out," Gerstenmaier replies good-naturedly.

Franz is quick to defend himself. "They just came for the women, and for a proper set-to. You could say it was a matter of honor."

"Some honor! Come close to losing an eye—all for honor. You're just an ass, and you're never gonna be anything else."

"When women are involved, the guys go crazy . . . ," Karl breaks in. "It doesn't stop at blows . . . . Everybody knows that, Ernst."

"Right. That's why I stay away from all that. Besides, the wife makes sure I don't do nothin' stupid." Gerstenmaier laughs.

"And what if they come after you?"

"Why should they, all of a sudden? I stay away from other women. One's plenty for me."

"You talk too much, and you talk about politics," interrupts his wife.

Gerstenmaier is stubborn. "Everybody around here knows what I think. I never tried to fool anybody."

Franz interjects: "What we have to say don't have nothin' to do with politics."

Karl becomes emphatic. "Today everything has to do with politics."

Gerstenmaier, his voice raised: "Why doesn't anybody say straight out what they're getting at?"

"Not so loud! You'll wake the children." His wife tries to calm him down.

Silence. Then Karl's voice again: "Now listen carefully to what I'm gonna tell you. I'm thinking of your own good. We're friends, aren't we?"

The gardener mutters something.

"In the village they're saying that the Jewboy, who's a real man now, has been seen one time too many with your Klara. And sumpin' like that—these days that's a political thing. All your fine talk won't change that, and the sooner you get that into your thick head, the better. If you don't, one of these days they'll come here, and then the fat'll be in the fire. Maybe they won't do anything to you, but him— they'll make mincemeat of him. I can't give you no guarantees here. Nowadays anything's possible."

I sit on the stairs. I feel cold all over. Down in the kitchen they're all talking at the same time again. I go up to my attic room. The stairs creak. I don't care. Let them hear me, all of them! I stand at the window and look at the blanket of snow covering the garden. After a while I open the window, climb out onto the slanted, snow-covered roof, and let myself slide down to the low shed. From there I jump down into the snow. In my bedroom slippers I run up to the vineyard and throw myself onto the steps. The bare branches of the apple trees stretch up into the empty sky. A chill shakes my body. Pollution of the race. Hideous caricatures flash before my eyes. Mincemeat.

The fawn whimpers and bleats until the blood streams from its slashed throat. I have no idea how long I have been sitting on the steps.

Finally I set out for the copse outside the gardener's retirement cottage. It starts to rain again. In an instant the first, tentative drops turn into a downpour. I take shelter in the hothouse at the side of the path. It stands deserted, the beds are empty. The glassed-in space is dim. The rain drums on the panes.

Klara appears from behind the early-ripening tomato plants Gerstenmaier raises in the spring, when the price is high. The shrubs stand in rows, tied by wires stretched between iron poles. It's pleasantly warm, here in the hothouse. You can work here without a shirt, your chest bare.

"What are you doing here?" Klara asks, pretending surprise.

"I'm working here," I reply tersely.

For weeks we have not exchanged a word. Always when she works near me, the gardener or his wife are there as well. Sometimes I don't see her for an entire week. But the more she stays away from me, the more she is in my thoughts and dreams, and neither prohibition nor fear can chase them away. It doesn't help to go into the city to visit my family or my friends. As soon as I return to the village, Klara is there.

I pick up the hose to fill the watering can used on the seedlings, as Gerstenmaier told me to.

She comes closer and reaches for the hose. "Let me help."

"I don't need help," I say with the utmost emphasis. She does not let go. We scuffle for the hose. Her face is close to mine.

"You afraid of me?" she whispers mockingly.

We fight for the hose, me pulling one way, she another. The water gushing from the thrashing hose soaks us until our clothes stick to our bodies. It seems to me that she is not wearing anything under her dress. I let go of the hose, grab her with both hands. We stand very close, wet and hot. With increasing force I slowly push down on her hands, until she kneels before me. We are breathing heavily.

"You're hurting me," she says, quietly and not at all angry. Our eyes lock. Become a man—now! There's no one here, no one will find out. But the terrible poison keeps me paralyzed. My youthful ardor dies. I flee the hothouse.

I hear Gerstenmaier's voice from a great distance. He is coming toward me, holding an umbrella. He's grown old, my gardener. His hair is gray, the curl is gone from it. Slowly he walks up to me and holds out his free hand. When he smiles at me, I can see gaps between his teeth. His goatee is gray.

"You made it—finally," he mumbles. "I always thought you'd come back." Holding the umbrella over both of us, he ushers me into his little house. In the kitchen, where the old white cupboard now stands, where the old square clock now hangs, his wife is waiting for us. Arthritis has affected every limb, and her long nose juts to a point from her wrinkled face. But her gaze is softer than the look I remember. Taking me by surprise, she hugs me. "Come, sit down and tell us how you're doing. I'll just put on water for coffee." Flustered and aimless, she crosses and recrosses the kitchen. The gardener and I sit down at the old table. I look at him and he looks at me. Not a word is spoken. I have forgotten what I wanted to ask him.

He is the one to break the silence. "All right, now you tell me. How could *that* happen?" He does not say what *that* is or what he means by it. He merely looks at me, his eyes questioning.

The word hangs over us, the way it came out in his terse farmer's language. And that means he is not looking for any subterfuges for all that has happened since we last saw each other. No excuses. He simply does not understand any of it, not the war, not the extermination of the Jews. He is looking to me for an explanation. And yet I have come here to get an explanation from him. He has no answers. And I? All the clever explanations I've heard and read are gone from my head. Simultaneously both of us shrug our shoulders and take a deep breath. Which means, What's there to say?

My eyes stray to the square kitchen clock.

With a mischievous smile he says, "Our old clock. Still loses five minutes every day, just like it used to."

His wife puts down a coffee cake, and Gerstenmaier takes the knife with the sickle-shaped blade from his pocket to cut off thick slices for each of us. We drink coffee, eat cake, and talk, at length and heartily. They ask about my parents and are happy to hear that they got out in time. I tell them what happened to me and all I've done. I also show them pictures of my family and of the kibbutz, of the mountains that were bare when we settled there in tents, of the forests we planted, and of the settlement as it looks today with its houses and gardens.

Here is the place from which I was expelled, and now I return victorious. In this moment I truly feel like one of the just.

What more do you want from us,
Land to which we have given our all.

Gerstenmaier carefully scrutinizes the snapshots I have brought. He holds them at some distance from his eyes and says with a note of respect, "You managed to get a lot done in the time you had. Here they smashed everything to bits. And you built something." Before I can say anything, he continues, "I know, you had all kinds of war too, but you won?"

I'm not sure whether he is asking a question or making a statement. I don't know the right way to tell him how many victims our victories cost us—us and our neighbors. Finally I say, "It's not so simple. Believe me."

Our eyes meet. He nods as a sign that he understands. "Of course I believe that it wasn't all that simple."

Our Arab neighbors from Abu-Sorek are the first refugees in the civil war that intensifies more and more the closer we come to the day on which our state will be established. One day about two thousand irregular armed forces appear, coming from the northeast, furnished with small arms and two cannons. They surround the neighboring kibbutz.

Once again the road that connects our settlements is cut off below Abu-Sorek. There is a rumor going around that a unit of Iraqi soldiers has entrenched itself in the village. The besieged kibbutz is under cannon fire day and night. There are also attempts to break through the security fence, but the attackers can be repelled. The armored cars of the Arab Legion stationed in Jordan drive back and forth on the road across from the kibbutz and shoot at it with machine guns. No one stops them. In the kibbutz there are the dead and the wounded, women and children among them, but the kibbutz withstands. It is almost impossible to bring reinforcements and munitions over the mountains or across the valley. Days of the deepest alarm pass. We can hear every grenade that strikes and explodes. On our only radio—we keep it in the dining hall—we hear the clumsily coded calls for reinforcements and aid. There is nothing we can do. In the meantime we deepen the defensive trenches around our kibbutz and debate whether homemade Molotov cocktails can keep the Arab Legion's armored car from penetrating the security fence. We hear that the British are preparing refugee camps for all those of us who want to save their lives. If we perish, what is to become of our children? We must not die.

> Do not say: this is my final journey,
> Storm clouds obscure the light of day . . . .

Another day passes and then another. Then, finally, organized defense groups come over the mountains and through the forests and drive the attackers with their cannons eastward. But the road between the two kibbutzim is still blocked off, at the precise spot where it is controlled by the neighboring Arab village. Suddenly we realize that all our hopes for good relations with the villagers are going up in smoke. The armies of the neighboring countries are getting ready to invade our still nonexistent state. Their governments are announcing as much. They will attack our settlements with full battle equipment. The connection between us and the other kibbutz becomes a matter of life and death. There is no place to which we can retreat. We will not become refugees again. Not we.

A few nights later we take our wives and children to a large cave in the hillside. During the Second World War we expanded it into a bunker, as a protection from German and Italian air attacks. In the cave we set up wooden cots; we take tools and medicines, so that should it become necessary, women and children can take refuge there. We take them to the cave when we hear that the neighboring village is to be attacked the following morning so as to liberate the road.

In the years since, I have often asked myself whether all these actions were really essential. The more I ponder the matter and take into consideration what we knew then, as well as everything we learned later, the more it seems to me obvious that we had no other choice here if we wanted to save our lives. "We have no other choice." That very quickly became the current catchword. Not everyone adopted it regretfully, as would become clear in the course of events.

At dawn three of us climb up to an observation post below the mountain crest, to the low stone wall that is the boundary between us and our neighbors. From here we will be able to survey the village, which is still wrapped in darkness. Tense and excited, we lie down in the grass, damp with dew. We have with us a small walkie-talkie, a new acquisition, with which we intend to inform our people down in the kibbutz about what will be going on in the hours to come. We have also been entrusted with all sorts of weapons, but we are to use them only to prevent a possible attempt to infiltrate the kibbutz. We have heard that the village is to be attacked from the east, from the other kibbutz, which has been liberated by this time. The chirping of birds announces the coming of dawn.

The first rays of the sun probe the sky above the hills of Nazareth on the other side of the valley. Dense fog descends on the village and wraps it in a fluffy blanket. Twilight.

And then: A shot, another. It is not clear who is shooting at whom. This first exchange is followed by all kinds of shots: single gunshots, followed by an echo; from time to time the rapid crack of an automatic weapon; in between, the dull thuds of exploding mortar shells.

We cannot see anything, only fog. Shouts in Arabic reverberate out of the white fluff. A donkey brays loud and long. A horrible howling rushes past above our heads—probably a shell fragment. Startled and frightened, we press our bodies into the ground. More shouts, more shots. Above everything, tatters of fog. On the slopes across from us a square stone house becomes visible on a rise, next to it a neglected little garden with some olive and fig trees. A fellah stands pressed against the wall of the house, his back to us; his hand holds a long-barreled rifle. With his free hand he signals to another house whose outlines gradually emerge through the fog. The fellah aims his gun around the corner of the house into the hillside. That is where tiny figures leap from rock to rock. We can also see tiny bolts of lightning spark from the ends of the black pipes they are holding. The last traces of fog float downward, deep between the flat roofs and the crowns of trees that rise into the morning light. The sun, like a majestic ball of fire, climbs above the mountain chain. An edifying spectacle.

> Hallelujah, praise God
> With harps and cymbals,
> All his creatures praise him,
> Hallelujah . . . Hallelujah . . .

I feel a great need to piss, a matter I take care of lying down so as to remain undetected behind the stone wall. Suddenly, directly in front of us, an armed man appears from a small hollow in the hillside. He wears a white kaffiyeh on his head, a black jacket, and white trousers that narrow toward his ankles. He runs along the wall that conceals us. A few meters from us he comes to a stop, his face turned to his village, and shouts something unintelligible. We squat on the ground, stiff and paralyzed. None of us would have been capable of aiming at him, even if we had thought of it. Now the man runs farther down the slope and disappears from sight. We use the walkie-talkie to tell our people that we cannot see anything except one fellah, who has fled into the valley.

"It was God's punishment," the woman says. "When they set the synagogue in the city on fire, I knew right away that no good could come of it."

The gardener sighs, but in an instant he is smiling his roguish smile again. "You can imagine how they pestered me all those years; they all knew where I stood. Especially at the end, when anybody with a brain in his head could've known that it was all over and there was nothing more to be won—right then they drafted me into the home reserves." He luxuriously relights his cheroot, which has gone out with all our talking. He slowly draws in the smoke and blows it out again with relish. "So, what's a man to do if he's made up his mind that he's not gonna die a hero's death? Now you see him, now you don't—that's what he does until it's over." He looks straight into my eyes, as he used to do in days gone by, when he tried to explain the ways of the world to the kid I was then. "But if they'd caught me, that would have been the end of me." He chops at his neck with the flat of his hand. "But you know what they say, it takes two to make a hanging." The echoes of long-ago days resound in his cackle. His wife, not without a trace of mockery, adds, "The French, they were looking for a suitable mayor. And guess who was suggested? This old dog here!"

"Your friends, Karl and Franz, did they at least stick with you?"

Gerstenmaier thoughtfully examines the ash at the end of his cheroot. "You know the saying, A friend in need . . . . Never have to say thank you to anybody—that's always been my way. Franz and Karl were drafted for rubble removal in town. They built a huge mountain, Mount Scrapolino, with the stones."

I do not inquire about the stones of the synagogue and whether one of the farmers might have used them to build terraces in his vineyard. All at once it seems to me no longer appropriate to ask the old gardener about this. Perhaps I'm afraid of his answer, as if my faith in humanity depended entirely on what he would say. I tell him that I am grateful for the patience he summoned up to teach me how to work.

He gestures widely. "That's one thing I managed, at least. I'm sorry to this day that you didn't get to like the idea of becoming a gardener. But putting up houses, that's a pretty good career too?" Once again I'm not sure whether he wants confirmation of his assumption or whether he has asked me a question. I am still trying to decide whether to tell him that after all the years of building houses in the kibbutz, subconscious yearnings to work with more than dead materials got the upper hand, when his wife says, "We never did understand exactly why you left from one minute to the next . . . ?"

"You afraid of me?" Klara asks. Her breath is hot.

I ignore the question and turn to the gardener. "What made you so sure I'd come back?"

"First, somebody from the government came and asked a lot of questions about your time here."

Restitution, I think to myself, investigated according to Hoyle. Nothing will remain concealed.

"So it was obvious you were still alive. Besides, a man, no matter where he goes, always has a longing for home. Am I right?" He smiles at me, baring the gaps in his teeth.

I am at a loss for an answer. There is no way I can agree with him, and if I disagree, I might hurt his feelings.

His wife comes to my aid. "Maybe you could say that a person wants to see the place where he was born at least one more time."

The square ceramic clock on the wall announces with a five-minute delay that it is time to go back to the city. They insist on accompanying me to the bus stop, armed with umbrellas and a large flashlight to light the way back to the village. When we pass the dark hothouse, I ask, "What are you growing in there now?"

"Not a thing," Gerstenmaier replies. "My son, Herbert, he thinks it's not worth it. Just imagine: the last day of the war a French pilot comes and shoots into the windowpanes, just when Klara was workin' inside."

Klara. I have no choice. I have to ask about her.

The woman: "Yeah, well, my sister . . . it's a long story." She falls silent. Her husband: "She could've died in the hothouse—and on the very last day of the war!" The woman: "Klara always had a mind of her own." The man: "Anyway, the French. When their troops left, those jerks yanked out all the phones and took 'em along to France." He continues with a note of bitterness, "Women with big bellies—those they left behind." His wife clears her throat as if to tell him to stop talking. Klara, I think. And do not ask. Better that she should live in my memory young and untouched by life. We go down the slope that used to be the gardener's vineyard. He sold it off an acre at a time as building lots to refugees from the East. He does not seem entirely reconciled to these sales. "The whole world's nothin' but a building site for refugees now," he mutters to himself.

"Today Germany—tomorrow the world."

The fog lifts completely and the village lies before us, deserted. Here and there wispy pillars of smoke rise from stoves and ovens that were so hastily abandoned. Down in the valley, near the road, a few dozen figures are moving—men, women, and children. They cross the road and assemble behind the low hill where the small domed stone building, the gravesite of a sheik, stands, the village graves around it. Not far away, at the edge of a copse of mulberry trees, stands a pump house. There they stop and look at their village, at Abu-Sorek.

No more shots ring out, here and there our men in their knitted caps come into view as they move forward cautiously from house to house. Explosions shake the air. Dust clouds rise when one of the houses caves in. Our neighbors stand in the valley, between the burial mound and the mulberry trees, and stare. On the mountain, I look down at them through my binoculars. I cannot make out whether they are talking to each other or whether they are silent.

A group of our people approach in single file through the fields in the valley, and later a few fellahin, their eyes bandaged, are led into the kibbutz. Shocked and agitated, we walk around them. We could have lived together in peace, until the end of time! They are led through the yard in single file, in their cloaks and worn-out shoes. They are farmers, just like us. The idea that people who have lived here for generations will not return to their own homes has not entered anybody's mind.

They have been brought here because we wanted to learn from them what happened to our friends, Bernhard and Gabriel, on the road below their village.

"What's your name?" our expert in Arab matters asks the first man.

"*Yah Khavaddya* [Sir]," the man replies from under the cloth that conceals his face. "I recognize your voice—and you have forgotten who I am?" Large beads of perspiration stand out on his forehead.

"What happened to our friends? Tell me!"

"We know nothing. People came from Yenin . . . . Maybe they took your friends along when they left. We saw nothing."

They are afraid of us, but they are even more afraid of their own people. We cannot get anything out of them that would tell us where our friends have disappeared to. Nor are they prepared to reveal who the strangers were who blew up the little bridge on the road so as to cut us off from the neighboring kibbutz when it was surrounded on all sides. The only thing that becomes clear is that the previous night the strangers, along with the rich men of the village, fled, abandoning the village to its fate.

Events shake us like an earthquake. We are confused and at a total loss. No one can think what to do with neighbors who have suddenly become our prisoners. We do not know what war is or how to deal with prisoners of war. Someone brings them something to eat and drink from the kitchen. They squat in the shade of young spruces at the edge of the yard and eat bread, cheese, and olives and drink tea. And we guard them, one of us armed with a gun, another with a cudgel. Our neighbors. They do not understand, and we do not understand. We only sense that nothing will ever be the same again. In the late afternoon, someone gives the order to lead them through the fields into territory east of the neighboring kibbutz. There are Arab villages there, and in all probability they will run into other inhabitants of Abu-Sorek with their families.

The following morning we repair the damaged bridge on the road below their village, and so the vital connection between our settlements is restored.

The conquered village stands deserted. Nobody knows what to do with the possessions that have been left behind and the abandoned cattle. The lowing of cows wanting to be milked, the bleating of thirsty sheep and goats are carried to our kibbutz on the east wind, as are strange odors. The following day people from the surrounding area stream into the village. Some take horses and all sorts of tools away with them. There is still no state, no laws. Each man is a law unto himself. We refuse to lay a hand on the possessions of our neighbors. Another day passes; then our people from the cowshed go over. They will bury the bodies trapped under the rubble to prevent an epidemic from breaking out.

In the course of time we hear that many of our former neighbors are living in a refugee camp near the small town of Yenin, about twelve miles distant from our kibbutz. Yenin and its environs later came under the authority of the Kingdom of Jordan, so that for many years it was far away, on the other side of the frontier. For a long time we go on believing that after a peace treaty is concluded, our neighbors will come back and reclaim their houses and fields.

But peace refuses to break out. Instead, the battles with the Arab armies, which invade the land from all sides, go on and on. Jewish and Arab villages and residential districts are vanquished and destroyed. The number of victims on both sides climbs into the thousands. A massive flight of the country's Arab residents begins. We will be discussing for years who is to be blamed for this. My conscience tells me that we bear none of the guilt. But we cannot hold ourselves entirely free of responsibility. One night, during a pause between battles, we see a column of buses drive by our kibbutz; they are carrying men in Arab dress toward the east, across the line of the armistice. Claims and counterclaims—the accounts grow longer and longer, become inextricably knotted.

Neither Here nor There

The bus takes me to the central railroad station. The open square and the main avenue are almost deserted. The lights of street-lamps and neon signs are reflected in the wet pavement. Wind. I go inside the railroad station and become drunk with the sound of voices and the clamor of echoing footsteps. I am overcome by the hidden tension of the place where people arrive, leave again, or stay, all without any definite purpose. I don't know what to do with myself.

I stroll past the booth at the end of the track where you have to prove that you are headed somewhere. I stare at the strangers, listen to the babble of many languages. One corner shelters the newspaper seller with the red drunkard's nose who is known throughout the town and shouts in his loud, penetrating voice, "Noo Zette, Noo Zette," which is supposed to mean *News Gazette,* a paper that went out of business long ago. A woman pushes her wheeled cart along the track and advertises her wares in a peculiar singsong: "Toilet water, fresh cakes!" When she says "cakes," her voice cracks. She also offers colorful postcards of the Swabian Railroad, pictures of an unscathed world.

"Help yourself!" a giant of a black American soldier says at the railroad buffet and shoves a plate of cheese sandwiches at his blonde companion. Then his white teeth bite into a red, greasy sausage, which he is holding in his other hand. His eyes laugh at his companion, and she smiles back at him. Obviously this is no one-night stand. I am not hungry and go out to the street. The big shop windows are brightly lit. Everything here is new, everything is rebuilt, including the large bookstore.

Holding my mother's hand, I climb the stairs to the mezzanine, where books for children and young people are shelved. Wonderful smell of printer's ink. All the secrets of the world are locked up in these books. *David Copperfield, Robinson Crusoe, Uncle Tom's Cabin, Don Quixote,* fairy tales by Wilhelm Hauff: "Fatima, or The Severed Hand," "The Inn in the Spessart." Magic worlds with goblins and ghosts, Oriental sheiks, and dwarves in green forests. And the fable of the Jew called Abner, who saw nothing and therefore must pay a big fine and receive a well-deserved beating, is there as well.

"I'm looking for a book for the boy, something that's right for his age," Mother says to the saleswoman. She presents me with a volume of Germanic sagas. The Nibelungen, glorious Siegfried murdered by the treacherous Hagen. The legend of Dietrich of Bern, for whom I have a special affection. I devour it all, even the tales of the princes and landgraves ensconced in castles clinging like eagles' aeries to rocky peaks that can be reached only by way of suspension bridges. From there they ruled the peasants down in the plain: Liechtenstein, the castle of the Hohenstaufens, who gave kings and emperors to the Reich. One of them, Barbarossa with the long beard, sits deep in the mountain and waits for the day of his return. I go with all of them on their journeys and campaigns, knights, kings, princes, and high stewards and their bold legions who ride toward their death on the battlefield, a song on their lips:

At break of day, at break of day
Death is galloping my way . . .

There is only one hero about whom I could never find out much. He lived here nearly two hundred years ago and financed the state's campaigns, his profligate life at court, his mistresses. His name was Süss Oppenheimer, and he was called Jew Süss. In the prince's name he collected oppressive taxes from the people, lived like a lord, heaped up possessions, and made his conquests among the local ladies. Until he fell victim to court intrigues and the ire of the people, who lacked the courage to rise up against their despotic ruler. The Jew was given a show trial and hanged, amid the howls of the crowd of spectators, in an iron cage at the top of a high gallows. That is what happened not quite two hundred years ago. Even earlier, at the time of one of the several and repeated expulsions of the Jews, one of the illustrious rulers called the Jews "gnawing vermin." I know nothing of all this. Nobody told me about it.

A few seignorial palaces around Royal Square, built in the last century, have been razed off the face of the earth. Others survive only in their facades. The wind whistles through the empty window cavities of the royal palace. The golden crown at the center of the roof is gone.

I let myself be driven on, to the round fountain where music lovers stroll on a Saturday, when an orchestra plays in the nearby pavilion, all the way to the still enchanted opera house. I climb the stairway, which no longer exists, to the tall entrance doors set between the classical columns of the facade, these too swept away, along with the cornice of Hellenistic statues that rims the roof.

"Get two pieces of wood for supports, I don't want the damn thing to collapse!" I am working for a contractor now, having practically fled the farm. For him we are putting up an outdoor reviewing stand between the lake and the opera house. On summer nights singers will perform on the staircase and the balcony of the opera house, gladdening the hearts of opera lovers with arias from Verdi and Puccini. Red signs with white letters are affixed to the entrances: Jews Keep Out. The carpenter whom I'm helping to strengthen the supports of the bleachers so that they will not collapse under the weight of opera lovers repeats his instruction to fetch some beams from the pile at the edge of the site. One of the tall side doors of the opera house is ajar. I go inside and walk down a long twilit hallway; on the ceiling there is a runner for moving scenery. A few steps more and I am standing on the huge stage. In the twilight I face a sea of empty seats. Gold-trimmed tiers set one above the other all the way to the ceiling somewhere up there. Huge crystal chandeliers hang down from the ceiling.

I sit down on a rock made of wood and painted burlap, I smell the glue and paint, and I stare into the space that seems to have no dimensions. Something nameless is happening inside me. The space is overwhelming; it draws me in. To be one with the thousand eyes staring at me. I am them; they are me. I am not allowed to stay here. Quickly I run back to my work.

From the plaza before the opera house I feel driven to the market square. Although this is the center of town, the avenues and streets are deserted. Isolated raindrops fall from the flat roofs of the houses that frame the square. They are built in a modern style, with straight lines, their windows tall and narrow. The new city hall gleams white in the light of the searchlight, its walls are smooth and practical. Little bells hang in square recesses at the tip of the tower. The building is smooth and beautiful—except for the pigeon shit that runs like a black carpet from the roof down the facade. The bells ring out:

> Be ever loyal and true
> Until you're claimed by death . . .

They sound from the tower. A stone gallery with statues at the four corners runs around it. Farther up, the tower divides into smaller towers with lead roofs. Four trumpeters stand on the gallery and blow their horns. Christmas carols float above the gabled roofs of the Old Town and its narrow alleys. "Silent night, holy night . . . ." Thick snowflakes dance in the gray sky and sink down on the booths of the Christmas fair, where they sell clothes and shoes as well as toys, cotton candy, and Turkish honey for the children. Thousands of lightbulbs in a cheerful zigzag border the gables of the old houses around the market square. Overnight a fragrant forest of fir trees grew in one of the side streets. In the same street shiny decorations and sparkling glass balls to hang on the tree are for sale. This is also the place where you can get tiny crèches, complete with mangers cradling the baby Jesus. Mary and Joseph stand next to the manger, and the Three Kings from the East kneel beside it. A little donkey looks out thoughtfully from behind the crèche.

He lies on the ground, near the wooden barracks that serve as our reading room. One day he turned up in the herds of wild donkeys that have roamed the area since the conquest of the neighboring Arab village. In time we carried off everything from there, the cows, the chickens, the horses and the rest of the animals, household utensils, and tools—everything except the donkeys and the dogs. They revert to a wild state. They run between the ruined houses, gallop along abandoned paths, under the fig and pomegranate trees. Snorting wildly, the ghostly herd of animals abandoned to their fate rushes past. Their clattering hooves stir up bothersome dust clouds, which come to lie on our souls.

That is how he came to us, the little black donkey. Nobody

knows where he came from. He has great difficulty standing on his little spindly legs in the middle of the yard. Possibly one leg is injured or broken. Later he stands by the grain silo and gobbles up seeds scattered on the ground. Nobody pays any attention to him. Only one person sets out a bucket of water. In the course of the next few days the children discover him and try to take care of him as best they can. They put a rope around his neck and tie him now to a shady olive tree, now to the pepper trees planted in the yard. They also try to ride him and to harness him to all sorts of carts. When it turns out that they cannot do anything with him, they leave him alone. Left to himself, he eats his fill of grains and hay, he slurps water at one of the faucets in the yard, and at night he finds a place to sleep at the side of the library. Nobody takes any notice of him. He is not one of us.

One day my three-year-old son discovers the donkey. He grabs hold of the rope around the creature's neck and shouting happily, he pulls him hither and yon. My sheltered child, for whom I am prepared to sacrifice everything, just to shield him from the horrors of war, plays with a little wild donkey that may, who knows, belong to some other child who is now living in a refugee camp farther east, beyond the line of demarcation that will soon form the frontier of our new nation. No one does any harm to the baby donkey with the spindly legs. Because no one sees him.

I do not understand what is happening to me during these hours in the deserted market square. I do not know whether I am here or there, now or then. Do not know why I cannot manage to be in one place, in one time. With all my might I make an effort to bring to mind the secure fulcrum of my life, a small spot in a province far, far away—the center of my world. It is the place I built with my friends, where my wife and our children live. It is as far away from here, from the nocturnal market square of the city that is so foreign and so familiar, as if it were in another galaxy. Everything would probably have been different if I had brought my wife with me and shared my youth with her. But she is not here. I cannot free myself from this city without ruptures.

Deeds and Responsibilities

"W e have to go into everything, down to the smallest detail, then we have to put it all together again piece by piece. We can hardly do otherwise. . . . "

She sits across from me on the other side of the table and looks at me with the understanding eyes of a social worker. She waits for my approval. Her eyes are beautiful, a light gray with green lights that flash now and then. Her thick, light-brown hair is pulled into a bun at the nape of her neck, as a strict schoolteacher might wear her hair. Only a tiny, funny curl dances loosely down her forehead. She is no beauty. But a small nose and soft lips lend her face a girlish charm, pretty surprising after a hasty judgment made on first sight.

"It's not something I can spare you. After all, it's the reason you came. Right?" Her last word resonates with a touch of a southern German dialect. I look at the wall behind her. No picture enlivens the smooth plane painted a pale, indifferent office color. It is as if pictures would be out of place in a room where life histories are put back together piece by piece. The window is closed. The warmth of the central heating dries up your throat. Through the open door to the next office I can see shelves laden with files, the same kind as the one that lies open on the table—my file.

How can she know why I have come if I have to ask myself what my real purpose is? There are plenty of reasons and arguments. Soap bubbles.

"If it's all right with you, Herr Fischmann, we'll begin at the beginning . . . ."

"Tamir," I correct her at once. "My name is Tamir, Frau Hofstätter." But why am I so annoyed?

"I'm so sorry. I forgot for a moment that you changed your name recently."

She's right. I myself have not gotten used to my new name.

She says, "If we're going to be particular about every detail: it's not Frau Hofstätter, it's Fräulein."

I am only now realizing that there is no wedding band on her long, delicate finger. A little embarrassed, I mutter, "I'm really sorry . . . my mistake." I look at my broad, strong hands. The wedding ring I have put on for this, my first trip abroad, on the thoughtful advice of my wife and quite contrary to our custom, makes my hand look like that of a respectable workman, a carpenter perhaps or a glazier.

"It doesn't matter," she assures me. "People can be different from what they appear to be at first glance. It's been known to happen." As if she has gathered new strength, she now says, "With your permission, Herr Tamir, we'll start at the very beginning. You were born in Stuttgart in 1917, the son of Michael Fischmann and his wife, Karoline."

A birth announcement on parchment paper proclaims the event:

Arnold Siegfried
It is with great pleasure that we announce
the birth of a healthy son.

Michael Fischmann and wife
née Defries

A sturdy infant on the fur rug, his head of black curls raised high, the lips expressing energy and a mind of his own. The eyes stare straight ahead out of the yellowed photograph. He is wearing a short shirt, and a bare bottom rises upward.

Toward the end of the last century Father, not much more than a boy himself, ran away from home, a small Galician village. His travels took him first to Vienna, then to Germany. He began his career as a tobacconist and worked his way up to ownership of a cigarette factory. Mother—that's another story. She was a child born late to a well-to-do Jewish family that had lived in the Rhineland for generations. There were seven brothers and sisters, who with their families came to make up an entire tribe, a splendid group portrait, the brothers in dark suits, chins raised above the stiff collars, the sisters in lace-trimmed dresses closed right up to the throat. Each woman wears a chain around her neck from which hangs a medallion or a gold watch.

Seven pairs of eyes look proud and secure. Dead. Suicide. Deported. Scattered to the four corners of the earth.

Fräulein Hofstätter's voice: "After four years in elementary school, you entered secondary school."

They forgot the public nursery school I attended daily, the brightly colored tin drum around my neck.

> With your foot you tap tap tap,
> With your hands you clap clap clap.
> Step out here, not too far . . .

I was not aware of any of the political disorders as the right and the left fought each other and fought against the republic. The nursery-school teachers showed great patience with the only Jewish child in their school. During the period of inflation, when a loaf of bread cost millions of marks and Father lost everything, my parents sent me to spend the summer in a camp run by Catholic Charities in the woods near the city. They kept us busy with games and told us stories about the life of Jesus. They also gave us cocoa and fresh rolls. My parents impressed on me, a six-year-old kid, that there was no need to make a big fuss about my Jewish heritage. I took their admonition to heart. Once, for the benefit of the counselor, I invented a story about my attendance at church every Sunday without fail. I'm sure she knew that the whole tale was pure invention. But she said not a word. When I entered secondary school, I discovered that my father was not a German citizen at all. It was only when I asked him to explain that he told me that during the First World War he had served in the Austrian Army. Later it had been suggested that he adopt German citizenship, but this, in his own words, he had refused to do, for reasons he was unable to explain. Galicia was awarded to Poland, and we along with it. Once again my parents told me that there was no need to mention in school that we were foreign nationals. Sometimes the mailman brought postcards in Yiddish, written in Hebrew letters, to our house. They were sent by Father's family in Poland. At home we did not speak of these relatives. Who we were, who we really were, where we belonged—that was shrouded in mist. Only gradually did I begin to understand that though we were not

among the old established Jewish families in the community, we
were not to be lumped with the Jews who had immigrated from the
East and who were for the most part poor. But one thing was for me
beyond any doubt: I felt—how could I feel otherwise?—that I fully
and completely belonged to this city.

"You went to secondary school for six years, and you stopped attend-
ing in 1933 . . . ."

"I was forced to stop," I interrupt Fräulein Hofstätter.

"That's right. That is what your declaration states. If I understand
the matter correctly, you intended to continue your studies but were
prevented from doing so because of racial persecution."

"I left school of my own free will."

Silence.

"Really?" She looks at me. Our eyes meet for several seconds, until
I lower my gaze. The Fräulein has a delicate throat that rises from the
demure neckline of her pale, plain blouse. Around her neck hangs a
finely engraved silver necklace with a silver pendant in the form of a
flower, a red stone at its center. My mother wore something very like it.

"They said: 'Jews don't want to work.'" I mumble.

Helpless rage rises in me. How am I to explain to this young woman
what it means to be compelled by circumstance and how the will is
born that turns this compulsion into a voluntary decision? If I claim
that I was a victim, and only a victim, what becomes of my dignity as
a human being responsible for his actions? But if I insist that I was
acting of my own free will, they may very well point out that I have
been blessed with the greatest prize that can fall to a person's lot. This
argument would relieve them of any responsibility. I am overcome
with misgivings. Someone enters the next room and calls out "A very
good morning" to Fräulein Hofstätter before turning to the shelved
documents. I think it's probable that they contain neatly written
records of everything that befell the Jews of the community. All those
who got away and who return now to claim compensation, and all the
others, those who were deported and gassed in death camps and cre-
mated afterward, of whom nothing is left but the names: Adels-
heimer, Adler, Baer, Baum, Bloch, Dreifuss . . . through the alphabet
all the way to Winter, Wolf, and Zimmern. Many of the names recall
German cities and villages where their grandparents and great-grand-
parents came from: Danziger, Dessauer, Frankfurter, Würzburger,

Wormser, Zirndorfer; as well as good Jewish names like Japhet, Kahn, and Levi. What remains of them are names, neatly filed away.

The young woman continues with irritating patience. "According to the documents, in 1933 you entered into a working relationship with Herr Gerstenmaier, a market gardener."

"I wanted to prepare myself for work in Israel—Palestine, as it was then."

"You left the job after less than a year. Herr Gerstenmaier testified that at the time Jews were not persecuted in his village."

My throat is dry from the central heating. I have no words with which to describe to this sheltered office worker the shame I felt when I was forbidden to feel and act like anybody else. Klara was no more than a pretext for my flight from a generally unbearable situation. The well-meaning young woman sitting across from me and studying my file can hardly understand the torments of a young man who was pulled this way and that between youthful passion and humiliating prohibitions. It is asking too much of her to expect her to grasp the inner conflict of a young man who is trying to free himself from an identity that is coming apart in order to find a new one that is unambiguous and whole.

"You must understand, Herr Tamir, that your request for restitution, no matter how justified it may be, must be investigated thoroughly and objectively . . . ."

There is nothing more for me to say. I should really end the conversation and leave. Perhaps she will continue to snoop into my actions and decisions of that time, will interrogate me as to why I returned to the city, worked on the building site, and left there as well, although, to all appearances, no one did anything to me. She will want to know how it happened that my parents and my sister emigrated to Palestine before I did, while I remained in this country until I was expelled. She is going to want to know every last detail. How I made out during those terrible years when the monster and his armies marched forward from one victory to the next all around us while the masses cheered him on and we tried to rescue the boys and girls who believed in us. Perhaps it was really my fate to contribute my bit to saving some young people. That is my fate. Why, then, restitution? Anyway, what does an individual fate matter compared to the Holocaust?

Not concealing my growing anger, I say, "That's quite right. Of course it's your job to inquire into every detail and to investigate it. And to do so with the necessary thoroughness." What's the matter with me? She has done nothing to deserve such scorn. But the words keep gushing from my mouth. "I must tell you, though, that this sort of investigation seems to me to border on bad taste." Now I am genuinely enraged. She may be capable of insisting that someone who has chosen to lead his life in the community of a kibbutz has already relinquished any claim to private property and with it to personal compensation. That, or something like that, is what I imagine her argument to be, without noticing that there has not been anything in her questions to point in that direction.

Fräulein Hofstätter puts down the papers she has been holding, and without looking at me, she says, "You seem to believe that this job gives me some kind of special pleasure." She gestures toward the files in the next room. "I know perfectly well that money can't make up for *that*." Without realizing it, she has lapsed into the local dialect. For a long time she stares at her hands, which are resting on my file. Then she raises her head, and our eyes meet without a word being spoken. Across from me sits the city where I sang along with the other children:

Open the gate,
Open the gate,
A golden coach is coming . . .

Bells are ringing. Across from me sits the city that expelled me and that is now ready to compensate me with money for a disrupted and poisoned youth. Across from me sit the girls with whom I played and the young women I was forbidden to love. A wild thought runs through me: If you are such a good person and want to compensate me for everything, why not with your whole being?

As if sensing that something is happening, she says, "I was barely seventeen at the end of the war."

Which is to say: What happened to the Jews of Stuttgart is not my fault.

She leans back in her chair, and her hand flies to the small pendant at her throat. "I was a loyal member of the League of German Girls, and with all my heart I believed that in the end we would win the war. Even after my older brother fell somewhere in the East. I don't care if you don't believe me. But I really had no idea what happened to the city's Jews. I never even knew any Jews. Even after the horrible facts became known, I refused for a long time to accept them, until it became impossible to close myself off from the truth."

"Your parents? They didn't know anything either?"

"My parents were good Germans; they didn't dare to think forbidden thoughts. Without realizing it, they were caught in the trap. They preferred to believe what everybody else believed. They didn't see the trap in time."

"Sure. Everybody was a victim. The hand of fate!" It's hard for me to hide my contempt.

When she replies, her voice is clear. "Of course I cannot speak for anybody else. But I . . . even if I don't feel that I'm guilty of anything . . . I do feel responsible." Clear and plain.

Her answer takes me by surprise. I cannot tear my eyes away from her calm gaze. "You? You were just a child when everything happened."

"It's a matter of conscience." She picks up my file, then lays it back down on the desk. "Let's leave it at that."

"All the same—a kind of guilt feeling?"

"No. No way. I said it before: I feel responsible. But if I do nothing to restore some kind of balance—if such a thing is even possible—then I do become guilty as well."

Strange, I think. I had to come all this way for a woman I don't even know to tell me that we have to try to set the world to rights.

She goes on. "When I work on a file like yours, I try to imagine the person and that person's life based on what I find in these papers. Often it's a depressing occupation, especially when I'm dealing with people who were compelled against their will to emigrate to some other place. People whose families have been destroyed and whose world lies in ruins. There are some cases where a word of consolation or sympathy would be like an insult. You're right: What I'm able to do cannot undo what happened. But at least I can try to be true to myself."

"Do you have this conversation with everybody who comes to your office?"

"After I studied your history, Herr Tamir, I dared to hope that our meeting would encourage me in my plan. You had a chance to start over, you found a goal in life: to build a new home in your homeland."

Her gaze rests questioningly on me. I do not speak.

After all that, how can I disappoint her, tell her that building houses stopped satisfying me as the years passed, that I have decided to give up construction and turn to the stage, although many of my friends consider this a betrayal of the ideal of work. Nor can I tell her about the visions of guilt that have pursued me since I landed in this city twenty-four hours ago. Here they expect me to play the hero. That's all right with me.

"I hope I've managed to live up to your expectations."

"As so often happens, I discover inconsistencies, in your statements as well, though polished and clear-cut statements are suspicious on their very face. In the end the ring of truth is what determines the decision."

"Your decision in my case?"

She sorts the papers in my file and shuts it with a snap. "It's precisely because of the contradictions and the instances that are not fully explained that I believe you."

"What are you saying?"

"The facts recorded here—I'm certifying that they're correct."

All of a sudden I would have liked her to ask me more questions, so that I can tell her what I have done in all those years since playing ring-around-the-rosy under the elms and poplars with the neighborhood children. All of a sudden I yearn to tell her how I and my friends built a new settlement, tell her who my wife is, tell her how many children we have. I want her to know what a kibbutz is and how we fought in the wars we did not want to happen. And why I am troubled by the victory over our Arab neighbors. I really want to explain to her why I feel no guilt but do feel responsible and cannot figure out how to translate this sense of responsibility into action. I would really like to tell her that what I want is to lead a simple life, without having to ask myself over and over who I am and what I am.

We end the official conversation in the Office for Restitution and go to a nearby coffeehouse. We drink fragrant coffee while I tell her a thousand and one stories, the way you talk when you want to avoid dangerous depths in the conversation. We talk easily and like friends, several times she laughs heartily while little dimples form in her cheeks.

Abruptly she asks, again with a hint of the local accent, "How'd it happen anyway that your claim for compensation was filed a couple of years ago but you didn't want to come though we asked you to explicitly?"

Instead of answering, I ask her, "How come a nice girl like you isn't married?"

She replies frankly, "Such a lot of men my age never came back from the war; I didn't like the others. Looks like I missed the one meant for me. But now I've made a life for myself in restitution. By the way: it's an impossible word."

We smile at each other like old friends who understand each other without saying a word. I make an effort—without great success—to put out of my mind this or that possible conclusion to the meeting with the nice young woman and to close a chapter in my life with sweet reconciliation. Neither of us gets up to leave. The increasingly long silences are beginning to speak for themselves.

Finally she pulls herself together. "You must have visited the new synagogue?"

I mutter something that can be taken to mean anything.

She continues. "You've been to the Jewish cemetery? The local government erected a monument to commemorate the Jewish community." Even before I can explain to her and to myself why I can't bring myself to inspect the monument or visit the new synagogue— because to do so would suggest that I am reconciled to everything— she adds, "Sometimes, when I leave work, I go to the Jewish cemetery. I walk around among the headstones and try to understand." She gives me a searching look, as if I had the answer. "If you'd like to come along . . . tonight?"

I seek out her eyes, and she looks back at me with a candid, calm gaze.

I sense that the time has not come. Not yet. Perhaps it will never come. I won't spend another night in this city, together with her, she and I, and each of us for the wrong reason.

I shall leave here, with all the conflicting worlds deep in my soul and with all the unsolved calculations in my heart. Restitution will not bring me peace.

❁

The Tangled Web of Places and Times

More than twenty years have passed since the day I first returned to my native city. In the meantime more wars and all sorts of events have passed over us, all of them recorded in the history books and none of them foreseen when we came here to build a home for ourselves. In the course of time the founders of our kibbutz were followed by more than a hundred sons and daughters, by youth groups from outside who had grown up with them and joined them, as did new immigrants from all over the world. Our kibbutz has become very large. And in our cemetery the rows of headstones keep on growing. The graves of Bernhard and Gabriel are there as well. Their remains were found some time after the war that was the first of all the wars to come. They were buried in a pit under the hillside where the neighboring village of Abu-Sorek used to stand, near the road. A monument of plain stones and a marble plaque commemorate the incident.

Today a powerful pumping station rises across from the plain monument. It is a component of the large waterworks through which the waters of the Sea of Genezareth flow into the southern part of the country. A hiking trail, which branches off from the road in the valley and leads to a picnic area on the wooded summit above, runs between the pump house and the monument. Thousands of hikers pass along it. Hardly anyone notices the memorial plaque on which the names of our two friends are carved. They were shot to death. Our neighbors saw it all and knew perfectly well what took place a stone's throw from their homes. A former inhabitant of Abu-Sorek, who was living in a refugee camp in the Kingdom of Jordan, led us to the spot where Bernhard and Gabriel were interred. So we could at least bury them in our cemetery.

For a long time we assumed that one day our neighbors would return to rebuild their village on their land. But as time passed, we grew more and more used to the ideas of our politicians, who believed that an understanding with the neighboring people would not be possible until after a peace treaty had been achieved. Only in this way, they claimed, could the calculations and countercalculations, which grew more convoluted year by year, be brought to a conclusion. In the meantime, we continue to build and expand our kibbutz. For a long time we have been receiving money from Germany as compensation for the loss of our families' possessions, for interruption in our schooling, for damages to physical health and persecutions of every kind. We decided to throw these sums into the common pot, and we have used them to build factories, so that our work could nourish our ever-growing settlement. We built a hall at the center of our kibbutz where we hold all our celebrations. It is also the site of our annual days of remembrance: one for our sons and friends who fell in the various wars, another for our families who perished in the Holocaust. The songs we sing nowadays are quite different from the naive and hopeful songs of the early days, before there was grief. We set up a memorial in our cemetery, six columns of the kind of bricks used to build ovens. Hundreds of names of family members are baked into these bricks. Names of people who have disappeared from the earth. At least, we think, the names will survive.

A long time ago we opened our home to young Germans, and we told them everything that had happened, and how, though we had no answer to the question of why. Sometimes we were astonished at how little most of them knew of their nation's recent past. Few felt any responsibility for the actions of their parents and grandparents, unlike the new friends we have since found in Germany, including Stuttgart, who openly and honestly try to come to terms with this past. Often we wanted to believe that eventually we would be allowed to forget, but to our great surprise we have had to find out again and again that memories return to oppress us and wounds we had thought healed gape open again.

It seems impossible to settle the account between us and the people with whom we share this region. Because there is no question for which we can find the same answer, we become more and more entangled in situations in which we would not find ourselves if reason and moderation prevailed in their world and in ours, so that we could come to terms with each other.

Well-meaning friends assure us that we have a right to exist, and they never notice that such assurances acknowledge that doubt is possible. If something is not in doubt, it does not require reassurance. I continue to ask myself why my existence, why our existence, must be secured at the expense of others'.

Recently I went for a walk in our woods with a friend, a young German, a photographer by profession, and I told him our story, what we wanted to be and why by force of circumstance we have become what we are. On the way we pass a spring that used to serve as the watering place for the village of Kiri. Now we have built a little park around the rock from which the water springs, in memory of a young man from the kibbutz who lost his life in a military accident. Near the spring we run into a group of young Arabs. With them is an old, white-haired man who is explaining to the others the significance of the small basin chiseled into the rock through which the spring water runs. Here the women of the village washed their laundry, the children bathed in it. We start a conversation with these visitors, and as we speak, it turns out that the old man once lived in the village and fled eastward after our comrades were murdered. He still lives in the refugee camp. We shake hands, and our talk is cordial. I ask him about his family, and he inquires into the well-being of mine, as if we were old friends. We both avoid mentioning the past. My friend, the young German photographer, can hardly believe his eyes. Hurriedly he raises his camera to record the meeting, as if to provide black-and-white evidence that it is not hatred that separates these two men, grown old.

Just another small, seemingly completely trivial, incident. But it encompasses the lot of all of us, lots that are enmeshed with each other. We cannot escape the tangled web of all the places and times. They are one.

So I sit here in my lawn chair, near our new swimming pool, and allow times and places to pass before me. I don't always succeed in keeping them apart, and each time, I tell my story in a slightly different way. But all the ways together result in one truth.

ARNON TAMIR
HAZOREA, AUTUMN 1983

Thirty Years Later: A Postscript

I learned just how difficult it is to tell the story of one life, or even a portion of it, truthfully—if indeed that truth needed demonstrating—during a second visit to the city of my birth, fifty years after my expulsion and about thirty years after my first journey.

This time I did not come alone; the trip was almost an affair of state. The municipality invited my wife, Elisheva, and me to come to Stuttgart for two weeks, along with many others from all over the world who had once lived here. We were received with a great show of hospitality. People from the administration and volunteers enveloped us in an atmosphere of goodwill, laced with Swabian cordiality.

Once again I ride the bus from the airport past the mansions along the narrow roads of the vineyards down into the city, and once more the memories return. But this time I can share them with my wife. Again the same street with the new, now already old, synagogue. We stay at the same hotel across the street that, large and imposing, stands on the site of the modest building of former times.

Again and from the first moment on, I live in a sense of déjà vu; times and events are superimposed in two, even three, layers. I see the city now; I see it as it was fifty years ago; I see the city I saw thirty years ago, when my memories took me back twenty years. Now all the times go through me at once, the present, the past, the long ago, as if I were looking at a multilevel chessboard with transparent planes and all the pieces, me among them, are being moved back and forth across the various levels simultaneously.

The city has arranged an ambitious program for us, with tours and outings; there is a reception at the city hall for us, where the mayor greets us with coy Swabian charm. We are led, we are driven, we travel through the landscapes of our childhood. We marvel at the city's newly acquired beauty. We are even a little bit proud, and we repress the slight uneasiness that tends to overcome us at the sight of so much efficiency.

It is hardly possible to describe the extent of the goodwill offered to us. The newspapers, the radio—all run stories about us. They spoil us with gifts, they shower us with thoughtful attention so that we will say . . . but what are we supposed to say? What are they expecting from us? We can literally feel their expectation. How can we say that this reception touches us deeply, that we look back to other times, many years ago, back where deep down a black hole of the impossible, the incomprehensible is opening—a hole that has never closed over.

There we go in large and small groups, old ladies and gentlemen, pleasant and well-mannered, each and every one having established a new life somewhere in the world. We are aware of the inquiring looks of the young German teachers who want to meet with us to learn what happened in the past. We sense very clearly their astonishment when they encounter polite and respectable retirees who remind them of their own grandparents, perfectly normal people. They look to us for the answer to their question: Why? We are supposed to explain to them why they expelled and killed us? They ask us instead of asking their own parents and grandparents.

Every encounter involves a discussion of life stories and events. What should we talk about if not about how each of us has fared? The stories become twisted into a thick cloud that hangs over us and accompanies us wherever we go. So we go through this crowded time, we remember, we suffer, we try to take pleasure in the good things that are offered us, and now and then we experience discordant moments. On each of our outings, for example, our group is escorted by a police patrol car. Somebody has seen graffiti scrawled on house walls that are reminiscent of the past. We read and hear about radicals who engage in terrorism. Better not to look into the abyss. . . .

After a meeting with the young teachers a man of indeterminate age approaches me and asks, "You don't recognize me?"

I have no idea who he might be.

"But I'm Kurt Gutmann. I used to live on the second floor, we lived in the same house. You don't remember?"

Of course I remember at once: his father was Jewish and his mother

Christian, and they had two sons. I introduce him to my wife and to a good friend from Stuttgart.

Clearly Kurt is delighted to tell the two women how, when I was a little boy, I used to come down to visit his mother on the second floor and beg her, "Aunt Alice, a plum . . . ."

Everybody laughs, even I. And yet I am embarrassed; I really was not prepared for such a direct encounter with my past; I would have preferred to regulate all the details first. And then this Kurt further claims that I had been a real little ruffian, fond of arguing with my fists whenever there was a difference of opinion. Though in some ways that recollection agrees with my own memories, I'd always seen myself more as a victim acting in self-defense, while his story places me in a different light.

Elisheva, our friend, the people around us, all of course get a kick out of these corrections of my self-portrait. Kurt says that we will meet again in the coming days, at which time we can have a long talk about everything. He wants to tell me every detail of how he and his family made it through the difficult years. Besides, he has another really great idea . . . . With these words he takes his leave.

Stuttgart is situated in a deep valley and is known for its hot, humid summer air. At night we leave the windows of our hotel room open. During one of the first nights we are awakened by the sound of many voices and the blaring of car horns that surge in through the open window. Not far from our street the racket is formidable.

"It has to be a demonstration to protest our visit," Elisheva says. "I'm sure. It can't be anything else."

"You're seeing ghosts." I try to reassure her, although I'm not so certain myself how to interpret the din that washes over us in waves and then recedes. "Who even knows about our visit?"

"It's been in all the papers," Elisheva insists. "They have to be right-wing radicals or Palestinians." We listen a while longer to the gradually diminishing noise and try to get back to sleep.

Loud conversations in Arabic, directly under our window, wake us. We are completely dumbfounded. Then there is loud banging at the door. Voices can be heard from the narrow side of the house, Arab voices. It takes us a while to get our bearings. The kibbutz project manager stands at the door and announces that this is the day when they will begin renovating our house. The contractor and his crew have arrived sooner than expected. For the time being we can stay in our quarters. A tall older man who looks more like a noble-man of old introduces himself in his best Hebrew: His name is Sammy, he and his two sons, who at the moment are unloading tools and construction material onto our lawn, work for the contractor, whose name is Churi. He smiles courteously and sketches a tiny bow in the direction of Elisheva, who stands beside me in her dressing gown. "No cause for alarm. Everything's fine," he says, lighting an American cigarette. He will repeat these words many times in the months to come.

"Let's have some coffee to wash away the scare," suggests Elisheva.

While the Italian waitress pours our coffee, we ask whether she heard the noise in the night. She beams. "Sure I did! Our soccer team won yesterday, all the Italian guest workers held a parade. Down the main street!"

"Of course," I say, "the play-offs, the World Cup."

I look at Elisheva. We are probably thinking the same thing.

On a rainy morning we gather in the Jewish cemetery. One of the city's top officials places a wreath on the memorial to the Jewish community and makes a short, moving speech. We stand in the driz-zle and look down at the well-tended graves, at the stone markers on which familiar names are carved. Once five thousand Jews lived in this city. All of them thought of it as their home. Half managed to emigrate in time; the other half found its final resting place in the camps. The mayor begs for forgiveness.

I banish from my heart the cynical saying, "The only good Jew is a dead Jew . . . " also and especially because in my country there are people who say the same thing about their Arab neighbors. The evil done by others does not begin to transform us into models of justice. Later we visit the old Jewish cemetery, the Hoppelau Cemetery. Rain is coming down in buckets on the eroded and crumbling gravestones, on the many Hebrew inscriptions. The first families were granted the right to be buried here a hundred and fifty years ago. At that time the cemetery lay far outside the city. Now it is surrounded by the roar of traffic, the Bosch Works are right next to it. We are told that during the Second World War the property containing the cemetery was handed over to the company so it could build more workshops. The company took over the cemetery and left it as it was.

A young couple, good friends of ours who live near the city, drive us through the magical landscape of the Swabian Jura, from the Urach Waterfall to the Blautopf, the lake shrouded in legend and hemmed in by steep mountains, which is fed by a subterranean spring with clear blue water. We recall Mörike's story of the Beautiful Lau and take pleasure in the sources of German poetry until—yes, until—we arrive at the nearby town. Now our young friend explains, not without a certain pride, that this is the place where one of the land's princes established a sort of university, thus making this province an early outpost of the Enlightenment. Unexpectedly I hear myself remarking that it was this very prince who had called the Jews "gnawing vermin." My friend is flabbergasted. I'm immediately sorry for what I have said. Basically, anti-Semitism is the others' problem, not ours. After my friend has recovered his composure, he turns the conversation to—what else?—the way Jews and Arabs live with each other.

We live in the midst of indescribable confusion. Lawns and gardens around our houses are transformed into a building site; bushes and flower beds have disappeared beneath piles of gravel and sand, planks and beams, bundles of steel bars and sacks of cement. Every morning Churi, the gray-haired contractor, brings a truckload of workers from the occupied territories—except on those days, of course, when a curfew is imposed because of the intifada. Sammy and his sons set up the concrete framework for the foundations and floors while the others dig, haul, do the simple work. Abruptly we are face to face: not the photograph in the newspaper, the images on television—no, the encounters are immediate, they take place next to the front door, under the window, around the house, from early morning until late afternoon. Yussuf, Machmood, Farid, Fahed. By day there are cordial greetings, we exchange a few words. At night we watch the incessant shootings on television, or we read about knifings in broad daylight. Since a number of houses are being renovated at the same time, the shouts in Arabic go on all day long. Most of the time a transistor radio blares Arab songs, and in every possible corner a finjan is brewing coffee. We know all about how to make coffee: for each cup, a teaspoonful of specially roasted coffee powder, flavored with a spice and a teaspoon of sugar; let it come to a boil. The secret lies in not pouring the water on too quickly, as the Jews do, but to let it come to a boil at least four times, until it runs clear.

We drink coffee together, we laugh, we ask about each others' families, and as far as it's possible, we avoid talking about the things reported daily in the papers and on television. At most, we reassure each other now and again: "Things will get better . . . ." What Yussuf or Fahed think while they are renovating the house for us they do not say. Nor do we ask.

I felt that during this visit, which might well be my last, I should document my origins for my children and grandchildren. With a rented video camera I filmed all the sites and places of which I have any memory. Very often they were new buildings, through which I saw the old, destroyed gabled houses. Since Elisheva had gone away for several days on family business, our friend, a native daughter of Stuttgart, came with me to the street where the house in which I grew up stands, just as it was, built of brown and gray sandstone, with bay windows and projecting moldings. A sign has been affixed next to the front door: Welfare Office for Yugoslav Guest Workers.

We step into the hallway. On the ground floor the closed door bears a sign in a foreign language. This used to be the apartment of the man who beat his wife, Claire, who had an illegitimate son with a Jew, Walter, and a son with her husband, Herbert, the boy with the gimpy leg. We climb up to the second floor. This is where Gutmann used to live with his wife, who was not Jewish, and their two sons. The door is opened for us by a dark-haired woman, a Balkan beauty. At the sight of the camera she flinches, but she relaxes when our friend explains to her that I want to record my childhood home with the camera. We continue up to the third floor. The fourth step from the top still squeaks. The wooden banister has also survived. The door is open; camera on my shoulder, my eye pressed to the view-finder, I enter the realm of my childhood with its old-fashioned door frames and windows bordered with molding. They fit precisely into the jigsaw puzzle of my memories, which I can never manage to complete. I step into my sister's room, where an empty office chair stands behind a desk. From there I go to the dining room with the heavy table and high-backed chairs, the sofa in the corner, and the book-case that holds all the German classics. In its place there now stand shelves loaded down with brochures in Serbian and Croatian. In the parlor with the mahogany furniture there are students' desks and a blackboard. On it is chalked: "Man (singular); men (plural). Child (singular); children (plural)." The next room was my parents' room with the wide double bed over which, in a gold frame, hung their wedding picture and where Tito still stares out from his aluminum frame at a row of computers. Across the hall my room, my bed, my little desk, and along the walls pictures from my childhood fantasy world. A young black-haired clerk smiles at me and says something in foreign-sounding German. A final glance from the bay window down into the street, the steeple of St. Mary's Church welcomes me from the distance. As a boy I slid down the lathe-turned wooden ban-ister and made my way to the tiny backyard, where we played soccer though it was strictly forbidden. Later one of my grandchildren will say, "Your yard wasn't any bigger than *that?*" What does that little smart-aleck know about the lost paradise? The piano factory is long gone, and now you can look straight at the rear of the houses all around, back porches, clotheslines—a panorama washed in gray, boring and monotonous. The eye snaps the picture; a new impres-sion on top of an old print etched into the soul. Everything present. Everything alien. There is no way home. There is no going back.

The camera leads me down the street along my daily walk to the high school. There is St. Mary's Church, quite near the school build-ing. The steeple, rising into the sky, signifies lordly power. Now I am no longer a little Jewish boy, now a Christian friend walks by my side. Why shouldn't I enter the high portal? We go into the church. My eye is pressed to the camera's viewfinder, and I take in this great silence. Light falls on the empty pews through a tall, tripartite win-dow. A little lamp burns above the altar in the corner with the statue of the Virgin. This is an empty place, lofty and empty. I look for the side entrance where the photographer took the class pictures at the end of the school year, the teacher standing at the center. The door is gone. It has been walled up.

We walk to the high school. The main door is locked. No sound or sight of any student. I remember a small side entrance. We ring the bell. A voice coming through the intercom asks, "Yes? Who is it?"

Go ahead, explain who you are, who you were, and why you have come here. Our friend answers for me. The door opens, and we climb the stairs to the principal's office. A woman of a certain age receives us. As it turns out later, she was the same nice young woman whom I spoke to thirty years earlier and who assured me, "No problem." Now she is a matron with a severe expression who looks me and my camera up and down suspiciously. The youthful-seeming principal appears; he explains the silence: the entire student body and the faculty have gone on a field trip. He is full of enthusiasm as he tells me the history of the school during the war and after, he assures me that today everything is quite, quite different. He returns to this assurance several times as he guides us through the empty building: Today everything is quite, quite different. Mixed classes, boys and girls. Different methods. Different teachers. If only they had not taken the gym away from him to use as a displaced-persons shelter. This, too, is a fact he returns to repeatedly. All this time, through the lens of my camera, I take in the marble columns and the marble arches, the black-and-white tile floors, the stone stairs, the wrought-iron railings. I smell the sour smell of forgotten sandwiches under the lids of the desks and the wax used to polish the wooden floors, which are now covered with linoleum. Nor do I leave before visiting my final classroom, with its view of the church clock. "Today of course everything is quite different," the good-natured principal says.

Finally he climbs a ladder and finds the yearbook for my class, which lists all the names, including mine, along with the year's-end report cards, all noted in Gothic script. The ledger also records where each student went afterward. The principal gives me a stack of annuals the school has issued in the course of the last decades. Later I will read in these about the hard times the school suffered. There is frequent reference to the humanistic ideals to which the high school felt committed at all times. I look for more. There is a brief mention of the fact that the principal, who had been tragically involved, was forced to resign after the war. That is all.

Genuinely heated discussions break out between us only when I discover that a wall they have put up is crooked or that the dimensions of a concrete foundation are not right. There are endless debates with the workers, with whom we have been living cheek by jowl for a long time, about whether it is really important to be quite so precise with measurements. Sammy, smiling broadly, says that it is not possible to judge a half-finished piece of work, there is no reason to get excited, in the end everything will be just fine. There will even be peace, one day, between the Jews and the Arabs. It will not do to take such a narrow view of things. I am not persuaded, and I insist on precise work. "But it's a building, not a pharmacy," moans Churi, the contractor. Surprisingly, he does not mind tearing down a wall or having a floor tiled twice, as if the material cost him nothing or he paid his people a pittance. Strangely, we do not investigate the matter further.

Exhausted by the wealth of impressions and tales, of new experiences and recalled events, we return to the hotel. The phone is ringing. Kurt Gutmann announces that he is coming to take us to his house tonight, he has a big surprise for me. All objections—we are too tired—are to no avail. Elisheva is exhausted, and so I am the only one who drives with Kurt to a suburb, to his little house, where his pudgy wife welcomes me. Kurt, whose great excitement I can feel, pushes me into a dining room chockful of furniture, where the seats are occupied by several people I do not know.

"Here he is!" Kurt presents me as if he were a master of ceremonies. Clearly he is expecting everyone to burst into cries of surprise. Two young people, Kurt's daughter and her boyfriend, are sitting on the sofa. For a while they listen to the old stories, then they leave. The third is Kurt's brother, who happens to be visiting. I'm supposed to have known him when he was a little boy. Now he resembles his father. He explains that he works as a soccer referee. Kurt introduces me to the fourth visitor, an older man with a friendly smile. "That's Herbert. The half-brother of Walter, from the ground floor."

What can any of us say? Four old men who sixty years ago, when they were children, lived in the same building now sit awkwardly in the same room and rummage through the trunks of their memories and actually have nothing to say to each other. I feel closer to the short, limping Herbert of those days than to this stranger, the retired man sitting across from me whom I have to ask what he did during the war. With a smile he points to his leg and assures me that he never came anywhere near to seeing any action. Kurt's brother goes into the next room to watch a World Cup match on television. After all, that's his business.

And yet: I do learn something new. Walter, Herbert's half-brother, the boy who had been beaten and tormented, whose father was a Jew, was taken on as an apprentice somewhere at the beginning of the war and somehow escaped notice. He did everything to join the army, though that was against the racial laws; and I am told that he did manage to become a soldier. "I'm absolutely certain that I won't come back from the Eastern front. But I have to be part of it," he is said to have declared. "He chose to die, in a way," Kurt says pompously. Herbert nods, smiling. Not a German, not a Jew, I think to myself, the only way to belong . . . .

The most astonishing story comes from Kurt when I ask him what happened to his parents.

"Somehow they made it to the beginning of the war and the following year, mainly with help from Mother's family. Although everyone urged Mother to divorce Father, she wasn't prepared to do that. For a long time Father was out of work, but then he got a job in the Office for Emigration in the Jewish community. One day—it was still before America entered the war—Father came home and said to Mother, 'Today a woman turned up in our office with two valid visas for the United States. If I marry her, I can get out of here. As a Jew, I have to expect the worst. Are you willing to divorce me?'"

I am appalled. "He left you, his wife and his children, to save his own hide?" I take it back at once. What a situation! He could guess what lay in store for him if he stayed. Nevertheless . . . . They say: Do not judge someone until you have walked in his shoes.

Kurt smiles weakly. "The thing about Father is, he was always a little bit self-centered. Always took the biggest piece of meat for himself . . . ."

"And the rest of you?"

"We survived. Somehow, as you can see for yourself. We started to work early on, and we wandered from one workplace to the next. When the deportations started and they came looking for us, we hid out with our grandparents. Mother's parents . . . ."

"And your mother?"

"What could she do . . . ? She was always loyal to Father . . . . She died soon after the end of the war. She never got over it."

I am deeply ashamed. After all, in the account of my first visit I wrote, "Gutmann's Christian wife . . . did she stick by him in the time of deportations?" Aunt Alice, I beg your forgiveness.

I reflect: Such an ordinary building, and so many fates, so many entanglements. Similar stories must have played themselves out in hundreds of thousands of apartment houses. I ask Kurt, "The neighbors? How did they act?"

"We moved away pretty quickly. We couldn't stay there. War really brings out people's true nature. Claire, for example—Herbert and Walter's mother—talked with people on Palace Square, and she kept saying at the top of her lungs that all the Jews should be deported and we should settle accounts with them once and for all. I understand, she had a personal account to settle with a Jew. But that—can you imagine?"

The day after I videotaped the house where I was born, my friend takes me to visit the Gerstenmaier family. Her heavy car drives over the shiny pavement of the wide road, which probably overlies the old cobbles over which I rattled on my bicycle. On both sides of the road there are factories, garages, gas stations, apartment houses. I can see hardly any fields. We arrive in the village that is no longer a village but a suburb, with mansions and apartment houses. We stop at the corner with the White Stag Inn. Up above, on the hill to the right, the church and the mayor's office stand as before. We turn left, but without the farms and barns and manure heaps to guide me, we lose our way. We turn back and try another approach. We drive through an alien suburb, no horse carts and tractors, nothing but polished cars on both sides of the street.

Where a sea of lettuce and cabbage, of bright flowers should spread out, a desert of stone and lumps of spilled concrete extends. We encounter an old man in a side street and ask him for the Gerstenmaier family. He mutters, "The old man is long gone. His wife lives on the hill. You've driven right by the gate . . . ." He points to a narrow wooden door. Above it, a sign: Beware of the Dog.

Should we turn back now that we have come this far? Cautiously we go up the narrow path under fir trees. It must have been the retirement section. At the top, a small clearing overgrown with grass and behind it a low, very simple house with walls crooked with age. The door and all the windows are shut. At one side there is a small green-house covered with plastic sheets and next to it a bed with mallows in full bloom and next to that a bed of radishes. Behind this, a few fruit trees and a half-wild garden in pleasant disorder.

The disorder around the house is total, half-filled ditches, clumps of carelessly spilled cement, wires, iron rods, rubber hoses, worn-down shoes, plastic sheets, wooden planks, a veritable chaos of materials and garbage. It becomes risky to approach the house after we have packed up our furniture and bits and pieces and moved out. Where once there was a large window full of flowers, a great hole now gapes. Here a little kitchenette is being added. We are sorry about the despoiled garden, which has disappeared under the spreading garbage, and yet our entreaties and words of encouragement cannot prevent the trampling of everything we have created in years of work.

"At heart the Arabs have remained a desert people," Elisheva says. "Look at their villages. They have no sense for ornamental trees and flowers." I, on the other hand, cannot understand how it is possible to work in such an absolute absence of order. Any attempt to talk to them about it is met with an amiable lack of understanding. "You could almost believe they're doing it on purpose! Even though we really get along pretty well," says Elisheva.

So we continue to drink coffee together, tell each other stories; and do not understand each other.

"No reason to get excited," Sammy says. "In the end, everything will be just fine." Looking at the confusion around the house, it's hard to believe him.

I call across the open space to the house: "Frau Gerstenmaier . . . Frau Gerstenmaier!" I am answered by furious barking from inside. The roughly carpentered door opens slowly, and in the door frame stands an old woman, somewhat bent, her face rutted with deep creases; I recognize the long nose. A few thin strands of white hair escape her bandanna. Her hand with the missing finger holds the angrily barking Pomeranian and calms him down: "Quiet, Spy. Quiet!"

I go up to her and say, "It's me, Frau Gerstenmaier. It's me," and I give her a hug, I kiss the wrinkled cheek, and she mumbles, "Oh, that I've lived long enough to see this one more time."

"Yes," I say, "I've come back."

The old woman invites us into her simple home, which smells slightly musty, of old age. Something is cooking in a black pot on the little stove. She offers us coffee, but all I want is to find out when her husband died and how the rest of the family is getting along. She tells me a long, sad story of illnesses and accidents, of land rented or sold to strangers, of the apartment houses that are going up everywhere. And only she is left, in the little house and the little garden.

"But I still work the garden," she says proudly. Her hands prove that this woman never stopped working, although she must be close to ninety. She brings out an album of faded photographs and tells my friend everything I got up to when I came to work in the truck garden. I was not much more than a kid, she says. I ask her if I may have one of the pictures, of her and her husband during that period, the two of them standing in front of the house, she wearing her apron and he in his old cardigan, his little cigar in his hand as always. I can hear his cackling laugh distinctly. After a while we say good-bye.

At the door I ask Frau Gerstenmaier, "And how is Klara?"

"Ah well. She's got all kinds of trouble . . . with her husband, other things . . . ."

I do not inquire further. After this visit we drive to the cemetery and, after a long search, find the grave of my gardener. I say good-bye to him as well.

Abu Musa is a specialist after my own heart. We have already struggled so hard with all the workers, with the roofers and tilers, the plasterers, carpenters, electricians, plumbers for the correct execution of their work within the time we agreed on, we have cursed God and the world for having let us enter on the adventure of renovation in the first place; time and again we have drunk coffee with everybody in friendship, although everybody knew perfectly well that in these parts agreements and promises have only a very limited lifespan. Then one day Churi, the contractor, brought along Abu Musa, a little old man, sixty if he was a day, with gray hair, always unshaven, his movements supple and catlike. Abu Musa's eyes are sly. His hands are

large and bony, their skin dry and cracked from chalk and cement.
These hands apply plaster gently and carefully to everything his pre-
decessors have spoiled. He smooths out, rounds off, artfully smears
over all cracks, slants, breaks with a mixture of sand, chalk, and
cement laced with synthetic. A cigarette is stuck in the corner of his
mouth; he takes it out only to clear his throat. When he has put the
finishing touches to each of his ornamental works of art, he smiles in
expectation of my approval. And it's true: What was crooked remains
crooked, and what is not neatly joined remains as it was; but under
the clever hands of Abu Musa it has turned into a postmodern masterpiece, brought to harmonious completion, a joy to the eye—a
man after my own heart. With him I can also talk seriously about
politics because he understands that what is crooked cannot be made
straight by force, and as long as one thing does not fit with the other,
some kind of arrangements have to be made.

The video camera leads me at last from the hotel across the street
to the offices next to the new synagogue. I make my way through the
electronically secured entrance into the offices on the top floor, ask
for permission to photograph the inside of the synagogue, with
which I am still unfamiliar. The man who is supposed to give me the
key happens to be on the telephone, he seems to be speaking with
someone from the police. I hear him say with pointed self-assurance,
"The minister has assured me personally that the police will do
everything in their power to keep anything from happening . . . ."
He looks at me as if to say, You see how I talk to them?

I prefer to keep my thoughts to myself. He opens a side door to the
synagogue for me. I take pictures of every nook, every detail, the Holy
of Holies, which is once again hidden behind a dark velvet curtain
with two lions embroidered in silver thread, the empty pews where
here and there a prayer book or a carefully folded prayer shawl lies.

The new synagogue is handsome, fitted out in good taste. Everything you need is there. The Tablets of the Law, the same ones that
used to stand on the railing of the old, destroyed synagogue, are set
into one of the walls. I look for the old high-backed pews, the
stained-glass windows, the large crystal chandelier in the cupola, the
Moorish arches . . . .

This synagogue is truly beautiful, but I cannot compare it with my childhood memories, which are slowly, slowly fading. . . .

Kurt Gutmann gives me no peace. This time he brings me a fat file. "I'm never going to leave you alone again," he declares. The file holds a correspondence spanning years. Copies of letters he sent and replies he received. Proudly he points to letterheads from the office of the federal chancellor, the minister of defense, the ministry of the interior, the judiciary, even the federal president. All the answers are couched in polite and correct language, and all assure him that the matter will be examined carefully or that they have not yet completed their investigation or that the case has exceeded the statute of limitations, that the facts are other than is claimed, that the particular agency is not the appropriate authority. The paper is smooth, the formulations polished like a crystal mirror, typed flawlessly.

Through the years Kurt has frequently engaged in controversies with authorities and officials, to object to the appointment of generals, government ministers, judges, and other officials who were members of the Party during the Thousand Year Reich and had once attained honors and riches; to go on record against the promotions and against the awarding of medals of merit and other orders, against bestowing the names of these same people on streets and barracks. He never grew tired of demanding that the victims and their memory be honored first. Not only did he send his letters to government offices; he also published them in newspapers, in desperate single combat. His letters and articles, which ran to the hundreds, slid off a smooth wall of polite rejections. Completely pointless, I think; I'm sure the man is known as a troublemaker . . . .

"You people in Israel should really help us."

I'm beginning to understand that he wants to recruit me for his campaign. I try to explain that facing up to their past is a matter for the Germans alone. All we can do is try to assume responsibility for ourselves and our actions, and there we have more than enough to do.

Obviously Kurt is not satisfied with my answer.

Thus the two weeks pass with meetings and discussions, excursions and memories, receptions and dinners. One night we return to the hotel from a visit to the opera. A nun, wearing her habit, is standing in the lobby. She holds a woven basket full of blackberries and blueberries. Stands in silence, her face unmoving, and waits for the Jews who used to live here to eat once more the fruits from the gardens of their youth.

What remain are the graves and the memorial, which recall a Jewish community that has disappeared from the face of the earth. What remains is the old Jewish cemetery, the final resting place of those who believed, a hundred and fifty years ago, that they had found their homeland here.

A. T.

HAZOREA, SPRING 1992

Afterword: On the Difficulties of
Learning from History

To live without having to keep asking myself who
I am and what I am.

Arnon Tamir was born in 1917 in Stuttgart. His last name was
Fischmann; his parents named their son Arnold Siegfried, pre-
sumably to express the hope that this young man would grow up to
have a successful career. Nothing came of it. To his parents' horror he
left high school in 1933 without graduating. Instead, this middle-class
boy, who had formed close ties with the German-Jewish youth movement called "Werkleute," began an apprenticeship with a gardener in
a suburb of Stuttgart. The young Jew was able to stay for only a year;
thereafter he was compelled to return to the anonymity of the city,
where he took a job on a construction site. In the city he was active
in the youth movement, trying to insure that as many of his comrades as possible would leave the country for Palestine. (His parents
and his sister also succeeded in emigrating there.) In 1938—Arnold
Siegfried was twenty-one at the time—he was arrested along with
thousands of other Jews in what was called the "Polish Action." He
was herded to the railroad station, packed onto a train, transported
eastward, and chased across the Polish border. He managed to make
his way to Palestine, a country he entered illegally, and joined the
Hazorea kibbutz, a communal settlement founded in 1936 near Haifa,
in the Yezre'el Valley, by a group of young German Jews, members of
the same youth movement.[1] Their aim was to establish a new, communal home, but it was built on Arab territory, among Arab neighbors. This refuge, no matter how isolated, was caught up in a web of
historical forces from which there was no escape. In order to save

their own lives, the Jewish settlers, many of whom were refugees, themselves became people who expel others.

In 1959 Tamir, now with an Israeli passport and a Hebrew name, returned to Germany for the first time, going back to the city where he grew up, in order to have his claim to financial restitution processed. More than twenty years later he wrote down what he experienced during those two days in Stuttgart. What was most important was his realization that he could not recover what he had been forced to leave behind and what he had lost. Not only had the place changed, he himself was no longer the same. There was no simple way "back." And just as, in 1959, he could not talk about his very different life in Israel with those he met (again) in Stuttgart, he did not immediately put into words what this new encounter with the city of his youth had meant to him as a man of forty. For that, too, would have presumed that all experiences were of a piece.

But before anything else, we are all alone with our own stories— and that means with our own suffering, doubts, injuries. The shock of learning this truth can still be felt in the words sixty-year-old Arnon Tamir committed to paper twenty years after his first return home. The many small "mis"understandings, which he records so meticulously, seem seared into his flesh. Tamir's memories are colored most of all by the strange reversal of circumstances. It is he, the victim of expulsion and terror, he of all people, the Jew who survived in distant Palestine/Israel, whom the German gentiles ask for an explanation of all that happened to the Jews in their country. They do not say, "What Germany did to the Jews." They ask instead, "How was *that* possible?" Their consciousness of their own history, the involvement and active participation of the Germans, thus remains unfocused, responsibility is shrugged off and masked behind a strange feeling of self-pity, which Tamir captures exactly; the small, revealing statement of his former neighbor—"Nobody cares about us"—is paradigmatic.

What characterizes this tale is the attention to unreconciled contradictions and to everything that makes for separations in a life in which the narrator is both victim and actor. No logical scheme underlies the alteration of times and places. So the story here is in the first place simply a depiction of the passage of time. But that sequence does not heal old wounds; it separates times and places from each other, divides people from each other, and serves to entrench existing divisions. One cannot return to a state that existed before such divisions, nor can one bridge them. The "journey back" does not lead to a beginning or an original source; but everywhere Tamir directs his attention and energy there are traces of the past in the present: "There is no escape from the tangle of all the places and times." The life of long ago does not simply lie "behind" the narrator. Arnon Tamir senses as much even on the airplane carrying him to Germany.

The man in the seat beside him, a German who had fought in Russia, intrudes on Tamir's thoughts. "That doesn't matter at all. Really it doesn't," he says when he learns that Tamir comes from Israel—in other words, that he is Jewish. *That doesn't matter*—this is usually the way we respond to an apology. So, from the perspective of his fellow passenger, the Jew must have apologized for being a Jew. But then the actual message is that Tamir, *although* he is a Jew, can safely return to Stuttgart.

Tamir's report does not stop with this observation of everyday anti-Semitism (as a gesture of ostracism, it corresponds to expulsion; it conceals the repressed factors of the man's own history). Nor is the traveler content with his new status, now a "safe" one, as a citizen of the state of Israel. Tamir gives in to the feelings the remark has awakened: his memories of the expulsion of 1938. That this is not some past memory, ready to be recalled at a moment's notice, but is instead a direct response to his seatmate is shown by the fact that the flood of images culminates in the recall of the detached observer, the train engineer, and of the people behind the closed shutters of the frontier town. And then the whole constellation switches around: For suddenly Tamir sees himself in the role of the observer. He, who "in the blink of an eye" himself became a refugee, stands at a specific point in his story on the side of those who make refugees of others.[2]

But the narrator *was* not solely a victim and refugee and *is* now a "citizen of his own state, secure and full of self-confidence, standing firmly on the ground of facts." The earth over which the traveler moves loses its firmness, it becomes layered and resembles quicksand. "Now all the times go through me at once, the present, the past, the long ago, as if I were looking at a multileveled chessboard. . . . " It is precisely this awareness that precludes a simple, straightforward narrative approach. There can be an "orderly, truthful" story only at the price of forgetting, only because it is a (practical) necessity to somehow mark the point of a new beginning: "I was busy, along with my friends, building a home for us, for our families, and for everyone willing to live and work with us. There was so much to be planned and done that we felt little need to think about the past." It requires two days in Stuttgart, the failed "going back" to a beginning that he had dreamed would be quite different, to recall the losses, correct the need to forget.

In this way Arnon Tamir's report documents the life of a German Jew—in decisive images and moments. What characterizes the memoir is not a smooth sequence but the simultaneity of unresolved tensions, the harsh juxtaposition of places, times, and events.

I first read Arnon Tamir's story when Iraqi troops had just occupied Kuwait and Saddam Hussein was threatening Israel with missile and gas attacks, something he was able to do with the technical and logistical support of the Germans. Saddam's aggression and Bush's intervention forced people to take sides; it was impossible for Germans to remain neutral spectators. Consequently a vehement debate broke out. The two sides were soon at irreconcilable loggerheads, not only concerning the sense or senselessness of military intervention, but more generally about the precarious relationship of Germans to Jews and Palestinians. I wish that at that time Arnon Tamir's report had found as many readers as possible among those who let events draw them into a hopeless confrontation and who believed that it was necessary for them to adopt unequivocal positions. Not because the book shows how to negotiate such positions or offers plain and simple answers to questions inevitably posed by the Gulf War. The account shows rather—and this, I believe, is what makes it so important—that such answers do not exist in the first place. Tamir's book demonstrates the emptiness of claims, in defense of one viewpoint or another, to have "learned from history": no lessons have been learned from balancing one guilt against another, from constructing historical parallels and smoothing over historical differences, from ignoring historical contradictions and contradictory reactions to them. Arnon Tamir's report takes very seriously the fact that the past, and especially the history of the Jews in Germany, is a very real element of the present; not only does he claim that this is so, but he also shows where and how this is the case in terms of what befell him during those two days in Stuttgart, which call to mind the story of an entire life.

As a rule anyone who tells a (his own) story does so with some hope of arriving at a "happy ending"; and even if the course of events is hopeless or catastrophic, then the story should at least be shown to have a meaning. The reason for telling it will thus be something like a lesson the narrator is eager to impart.

But Arnon Tamir has no interest whatsoever in this objective. For every encounter, every occurrence he relates, another one runs counter to it. Even at the risk of steering his story into stormy waters beyond the safe haven of a temporal-spatial order, Tamir's account resolutely continues its motion and countermotion. Even before any standpoint can be certified by reference to an experience made or an ordeal survived, Tamir expresses something that puts the lie to unequivocal positions. By his method of storytelling, Arnon Tamir shows how, even under the force of events that compel the adoption of a particular stance, it is possible to avoid the danger of becoming rigid and unyielding, entrenched in the choices defined by the necessity of the historical moment. Events, experiences, and knowledge do not ossify into "ordinary solutions" because Arnon Tamir and his story hold fast to the painful experience that sequential and simultaneous events and experiences, even contradictory events and experiences, cannot be shaped into a homogeneous whole.

This does not in any way amount to relativism and resignation. But it does bear witness to a sense of reality and worldly wisdom. And it attests to a great power of memory: Tamir's "journey back" is not a search for a safe haven when his own and others' experiences, when his own and others' suffering, threaten to overwhelm him.

Seen from this perspective, the journey is an exceptional situation: The traveler seems to move freely *between* places, *between* points in time; he also seems to have been set free from the pragmatic constraints of everyday life, which can necessitate the absence of ambiguity. But this "freedom" is deceptive. It is the freedom of the homeless. Arnon Tamir writes: "I do not know whether I am here or there, now or then. Do not know why I cannot manage to be in one place, in one time." Anyone who questions in this way is writing, if I am allowed to sound dramatic, for his life. He needs to communicate something so that he (together with others) can hold on to it.

How hard this is is shown by the dialogue with the social worker, which follows Tamir's acknowledgment of how time and place have collapsed in his memory. She wants to recapitulate and reconstruct his life—and that is exactly what will not help. For it would result in the kind of history that has always been written, as it were, officially. Against such a background, with the help of questionnaires and checks for consistency, the course a life has taken would be fixed once and for all. The claimant must decide: perpetrator or victim? Such a firm definition might suffice for the files, might meet some pragmatic requirement; it may even be that it can become the vantage point that, for the moment, provides order and calm, a sense of direction. But those involved—like anyone who resorts to such a position— lose something: the experience of the foreign.

There is a moment when the claimant and the bureaucrat take each other by surprise, when they shed their established expectations and roles: Tamir averts with scorn and contempt what he expects to hear from her, and she counters with the "clear and plain" sentence, "I do feel responsible." Here it seems possible, for a brief instant, to look through one's own history at the other's, the foreign history. Not guilt but responsibility.

Because Arnon Tamir succeeds in keeping his narrative open to such contrary movements, something can, after all, be learned from (this) history. This ability presupposes a feeling for divisiveness, for alienation, and for barriers to understanding. It has its roots in a wound received early in life.

In 1917 Arnon Tamir was born in Stuttgart under the name of Arnold Siegfried Fischmann. The Fischmanns were a solidly middle-class family. Their life was barely distinguishable from that of their "German" neighbors. They observed the Jewish holidays, were members of the Jewish community (five thousand Jews lived in Stuttgart in the 1920s, only about half of whom escaped the Holocaust), attended the synagogue where, on its inauguration, the rabbi had called out, "Hail to you, Stuttgart, our Jerusalem"—that is how much the Jews felt at home in this city.

However, the Fischmanns were not true citizens of Stuttgart. Arnold's mother was born in the Rhineland into an extended, well-to-do Jewish family that had spread throughout the country. His father, on the other hand, came from Galicia, which was Austrian until 1918 and thereafter belonged to Poland; in other words, he was an "Eastern Jew." He worked his way up from tobacco worker to owner of a cigarette factory. But the family history was never mentioned. Not in the community, because there, as elsewhere, Eastern Jews were not held in great esteem. Not in nursery school and not in elementary school, where young Arnold was "at times the only Jew."[3] Thus he had to read the history of his ancestors from between the lines of silence and camouflage; it too was a history of separations, of place changes, of veiled identities.

What undoubtedly made an impression was the timeworn Jewish experience that there are always "more powerful people" somewhere who will come and turn neighbors into strangers, into enemies. These are the words Arnon Tamir will hear from his Arab neighbors in the years between 1938 and 1948; as a boy, he had learned the same lesson from his parents.

Like many of his Jewish contemporaries, Arnold Fischmann cannot find a ground on which to "settle" (in the metaphoric sense of the word). Nevertheless, Arnon Tamir writes, "I felt—how could I feel otherwise?—that I belonged to this city completely." He was driven out of this city—the city where, as a member of the German-Jewish youth movement, he had dreamed of a new beginning, a new life.

The point of reference for these dreams was Germany. His hope was to realize something that had been withheld from Jews in their long history (and not only in Germany): to settle. Settling means not only property but self-sufficiency, gainfully working the land. That idea is also signaled in the name of the group of which Arnold Fischmann became a member: "Werkleute." Moni Alon, one of the cofounders of the Hazorea kibbutz, remarks, "Life in the kibbutz not only seemed to us a necessity, in order to create new settlements and to persuade Jews from the large Western cities to take up manual labor, but it also seemed to us a kind of realization of the socialism that not only was supposed to seize whole countries at some later time but that we wanted to realize in a very personal way in our lives." Meir Nehab, also a member of Hazorea, recalls, "We believed at first: What we want to realize we must do in Germany. But after the boycott we understood: There is no future for us in Germany. And we concluded, actually quite logically and consistently: We'll make a kibbutz in Palestine."4

Arnon Tamir, wandering the streets of the city that once was his home, also recalls the shock of the boycott day, the blockade of Jewish stores by the Brownshirts on April 1, 1933. "Fair game. I'm the one who can be denied the right to live in this world." This terror traveled with him, as it did with so many other Jews, to Palestine—to Israel.

The Jewish youth movement was not entirely Zionist in orientation; we must remember this fact as we follow Arnon Tamir's tales from Hazorea. But after 1933, when anti-Semitism became a government directive, the Zionist tenets of the impossibility of assimilation and the inevitability of anti-Semitism were confirmed with gruesome consistency. The Zionist objectives—emigration to Palestine, establishment of a state belonging to the Jews—inevitably appeared to be the only effective response to the Nazi threat.

Jakov Lind's *Selbstporträt,* however, shows the reservations many young Jews had about the Zionist idea of a state (reservations that also characterize Arnon Tamir's story, which takes as its political point of reference life in the Hazorea kibbutz). "*Jews out of here?* The Zionists have been vociferous in calling for exactly the same thing, ever since Theodor Herzl demanded a state of their own for the Jews. . . . We belong in Palestine, wherever that may be. If Hungarians, Poles, Slovenians, and Czechs need a state of their own, where they can manage their own affairs, then Jews also need a state. Long before the Nazis, there was a Zionist movement. A Jew could choose between being a victim and 'master of his fate.'"5

Time and again the same "either/or" arose. In her history of Palestine, Susann Heenen-Wolff writes: "Many people who had escaped death in German concentration camps ended up in Palestine/Israel and saw themselves threatened once more, the only difference being that this time they had weapons at their disposal. Countless autobiographies, memoirs, and novels reveal that many Jews *experienced* a kind of continuity, even if this was contradicted by historical reality."6 In Arnon Tamir's account we can sense the effort required to avoid this experience, to counter the compulsion to accept such a continuity.

"'We have no other choice.' That very quickly became the current catchword. Not everyone adopted it regretfully." And regret alone would not be enough to lessen historical compulsions; they would only be reinforced, and the perpetrator would then justify his actions by describing himself as their victim.

"Visions of guilt" pursue the man who has returned to his first home and to the place of his youthful dreams. It was also a place of humiliation, where an identity that was already broken finally "shattered." And here the wish was born "to find a new one, whole and unbroken." And therefore this was also the place where an endless sequence of "accounts and counteraccounts" might have arisen in Tamir's history, the kind of sequence we are accustomed to hearing told as history. But Arnon Tamir tells his story in a different way; he narrates with an awareness of his responsibility for a piece of history in which he had a part. Thus the story anticipates something: the utopia of a form of history that is created consciously, in which it is no longer "decided somewhere that strength must be demonstrated," so that you can successfully present your accounting.

That it is still necessary for Jews in Israel to make a show of strength is not something Tamir forgets; that, too, is part of the responsibility of the narrator, who has had to learn that "the juxtaposition of utopia and what is called reality" must be continued. Juxtaposition cannot mean setting one against the other so as to play utopia off against reality and use one to slay the other. The presupposition instead must be that we can tolerate the existence of mutually irreconcilable matters. There is no other way to break the chain of calculation and countercalculation.

That is the conclusion of Arnon Tamir's story. It was difficult for me to accept. My problem may be related to the fact that I could have been one of the two boys Arnon Tamir noticed on the bus going to the gardener's village in 1959: "Both of the students look out of the window at the passing fields. It is their country, their home. No one would think of contesting this fact, even if their country is still occupied by foreign soldiers. Even after a lost war they are safe." Twenty years ago, even ten years ago, I would have vehemently denied that the fact that this "beautiful country" is our country, is my country, was of any significance—and to this day I feel all too frequently that

I can happily do without that country. But—and this is what I ignored until now—that is quite beside the point. Rather, the point is that my feeling of otherness was never linked to a profound insecurity, to a sense of having no rights under the law. I never found myself in the position of having to explain or justify my existence to anyone. But that is precisely the constraint that determined the life of Arnon Tamir, who was expelled from Germany as a Jew, who joined a kibbutz, and who became a citizen of the state of Israel. This is what makes his personal history so different from mine. In a very specific way, Arnon Tamir's report points to this difference, to what distinguishes between us and separates us. By telling his story, he refers me to the history for which I also bear some responsibility.

KLAUS BINDER

FRANKFURT AM MAIN, APRIL 1992

Notes

1. A valuable account of the history of the Hazorea kibbutz is *Die rettende Kraft der Utopie: Deutsche Juden gründen den Kibbuz Hasorea*, edited by W. G. Godenschweger and F. Vilmar (Frankfurt am Main, 1990). In this context I would also like to call the reader's attention to Arthur Koestler's novel *Thieves in the Night: Chronicle of an Experiment* (New York, 1946). This moving narrative recounts the story of a kibbutz in the political and social situation in Palestine shortly before the establishment of the state of Israel. Susann Heenen-Wolff, in *Erez Palästina: Juden und Palästinenser im Konflikt um ein Land*, Sammlung Luchterhand 945 (Frankfurt am Main, 1990), gives a brief account of the Palestinian conflict, brought to life by the inclusion of many documents, especially biographies. A very graphic view of daily life in Palestine in the years 1935–41 is given in Walter Zadek, *Kein Utopia: Araber, Juden, Engländer in Palästina. Fotografien* (Berlin, 1986).

2. In his short history of the Hazorea kibbutz, Jacob Michaeli writes of the military confrontations around Hazorea in the "first civil war": "Early in 1948 the neighboring kibbutz, Mishmar Ha'emek, was surrounded by the troops of Kauki [the commander of an Iraqi

liberation army, three battalions with artillery]. Overnight Hazorea became the frontier kibbutz. Two members of the kibbutz disappeared. . . . The bodies were not found for years. After the double murder the inhabitants of the surrounding Arab villages, in spite of the cordial relations with us up to that time, fled to the area near Yenin. The land that belonged to them was later . . . acquired by the Hazorea kibbutz (what was involved was the Miri ground, the common family property of the village according to Ottoman law)." See also Godenschweger and Vilmar, *Die rettende Kraft der Utopie,* 150.

3. Arnon Tamir reports on this and—though only briefly—on the history of the Jewish community in Stuttgart in the video mentioned in his postscript, which he filmed for his grandchildren during his 1990 trip to Stuttgart.

4. See Godenschweger and Vilmar, *Die rettende Kraft der Utopie,* 66, 64.

5. Jakov Lind, *Selbstporträt* (Frankfurt am Main, 1970); quoted in Heenen-Wolff, *Erez Palästina,* 54.

6. Heenen-Wolff, *Erez Palästina;* see pages 83–84.

❖

Jewish Lives